EMBRACING YOUR IDENTITY IN CHRIST:

Discovering Your True Worth And Purpose

BY RENE COLEMAN

Table of Contents

Introduction: There Is Hope... 8

Chapter 1 14

Embracing Your Identity in God: A Journey to Purpose 14

The Importance of Identity in Christ: Finding True Worth Beyond Societal Pressures 14

Embracing Our Identity in Christ: 15

Overcoming Societal Pressures: 21

Finding True Worth in God: 26

The Freedom to Be Authentic: 30

Chapter 2 37

Uncovering the Lies: Challenging False Beliefs about Self-Worth 37

Identifying Common Misconceptions and Lies: 38

Examining the Impact of Comparison, Perfectionism, and Insecurity: 40

Challenging the Lies and Cultivating True Self-Worth: 41

Chapter 3 45

Embracing God's Love: Discovering the Depth of His Unconditional Love 45

Exploring the Nature of God's Love: 46

Healing Past Wounds through God's Love: 47

Embracing the Transformative Power of God's Love: 49

Chapter 4 52

Healing Past Wounds and Developing a Healthy Self-Image through God's Love 52

God's Design: Uniquely Created for a Purpose 52

Healing Past Wounds and Developing a Healthy Self-Image 54

Chapter 5 66

God's Design: Uniquely Created for a Purpose 66

Recognizing that Each Woman is Fearfully and Wonderfully Made: 66

Practical exercises   69

Here are some scriptures that reinforce the importance of avoiding comparison and embracing our identity in God. *These can be used in prayer*: 75

Discovering and Embracing Personal Gifts, Talents, and Passions: 78

Chapter 6   82

Finding Purpose: Seeking God's Will for Your Life   82

Seeking Guidance through Prayer, Scripture, and Discernment: 83

Here are some scriptures that emphasize the importance of seeking and finding purpose in God: 84

Understanding that Purpose Unfolds in Seasons: 87

Chapter 7   90

Overcoming Obstacles: Navigating Challenges to Your Identity   90

Addressing Common Obstacles: Self-Doubt, Fear, and Failure   91

Self-Doubt   91

Fear   94

Failure 97

Developing Resilience and Faith in God's Plan during Difficult Times 100

To actively seek God's guidance, consider implementing these practices: 112

Chapter 8   116

Walking in Confidence: Stepping into Your True Identity 116

Cultivating a Healthy Self-Esteem Grounded in Christ's Love: 117

Embracing God's Promises and Living Boldly for His Glory: 131

Chapter 9   141

Living a Purposeful Life: Impacting Others for God's Kingdom   141

Discovering How Our Unique Purpose Aligns with God's Kingdom Work: 142

Practical Ways to Serve, Inspire, and Influence Others through Our Identity in Christ: 151

Chapter 10   168

Sustaining Your Identity: Nurturing a Lifelong Journey   168

Cultivating Daily Habits and Spiritual Disciplines: 169

Surrounding Yourself with a Supportive Christian Community: 172

Chapter 11   179

The Importance of Knowing Your Identity in Christ and Its Impact on Healing from Trauma and Finding Purpose 179

The Identity in Christ: 180

Healing from Trauma: 180

Finding Purpose: 182

Living a Purpose-Filled Life: 184

The Identity in Christ: 185

Chapter 12   191

Living with Confidence and Purpose   191

Summarizing Key Lessons and Takeaways: 191

Embracing Your Identity in Christ and Stepping into Your God-given Purpose: 195

Chapter 13   198

Seeking God's Will: Stepping into Your True Identity   198

The Importance of Seeking God's Will: 198

Listening to God's Voice: 199

Discerning God's Will: 200

Practical Exercises for Seeking God's Will: 200

As We Close...   203

INTRODUCTION: THERE IS HOPE...

Dear reader,

Welcome to the beginning of an incredible journey—a journey of self-discovery, healing, and purpose. Whether you are a man or a woman, young or old, this book is an invitation for you to embark on a transformative adventure of embracing your identity in God and stepping into your purpose.

In a world filled with noise, distractions, and competing voices telling us who we should be and what we should strive for, it is easy to lose sight of our true identity. We often find ourselves caught up in the pressures of society, comparison, and the relentless pursuit of worldly success. But deep within our hearts, there is a longing for something more—something authentic, fulfilling, and meaningful.

This book is an invitation to reconnect with the core of who you are—a beloved child of God, fearfully and wonderfully made with unique gifts, talents, and passions. It is an invitation to discover the purpose for which you were created and to live a life that brings glory to God and fulfillment to your soul.

As you journey through the pages of this book, I encourage you to approach it with an open heart, a receptive mind, and a willingness to explore the depths of your identity in God. Leave behind any preconceived notions, doubts, or fears, and allow yourself to fully engage with the material presented.

In the chapters that follow, you will find profound insights, practical exercises, and biblical teachings carefully crafted to guide you towards a deeper understanding of your true identity and purpose. Each chapter is designed to gently peel away the layers of societal conditioning, self-doubt, and past hurts, leading you towards a place of healing, wholeness, and confidence.

You are not alone on this journey. Together, we will explore the significance of embracing our identity in God, challenge the false beliefs that hinder self-worth, uncover the depth of God's unconditional love, and heal the wounds that have shaped our self-perception. We will seek God's will, overcome obstacles, and learn to walk in confidence, impacting others for His Kingdom.

I want you to know that wherever you are in your journey—whether you feel lost, broken, or simply seeking greater clarity—there is hope.

God has a unique purpose for your life, and He desires to lead you into a life of significance and impact. He is with you every step of the way, ready to guide, comfort, and empower you.

So, dear reader, I invite you to take this journey with me. Let us embark on a path of self-discovery, healing, and purpose together. May you approach this book with a spirit of curiosity, openness, and anticipation for what lies ahead. I pray that as you embrace your identity in God and step into your purpose, you will experience a profound transformation that will ripple through every aspect of your life.

Are you ready? Let's begin this adventure of a lifetime.

With love and hope,

Rene

CHAPTER 1

EMBRACING YOUR IDENTITY IN GOD: A JOURNEY TO PURPOSE

THE IMPORTANCE OF IDENTITY IN CHRIST: FINDING TRUE WORTH BEYOND SOCIETAL PRESSURES

In a world that constantly bombards us with messages about what defines our worth, it is crucial to discover and embrace our identity in Christ. Our true worth is not found in material possessions, social status, or external achievements, but in the unchanging love and acceptance of our Creator. In this chapter, we will explore the significance of embracing our identity in Christ and discuss how it empowers us to overcome societal pressures and find our true worth in God.

EMBRACING OUR IDENTITY IN CHRIST:

Our identity in Christ is rooted in the unchanging truth that we are loved, chosen, and valued by God. Understanding and embracing this truth is transformative and life-giving. When we accept Christ as our Savior, we become new creations, adopted into God's family, and co-heirs with Christ (2 Corinthians 5:17, Galatians 4:7). Our identity is no longer defined by our past mistakes, shortcomings, or the world's standards, but by our relationship with Him.

In the depths of our souls, there is a longing for a sense of purpose, worth, and belonging. We often seek these things in the fleeting pleasures and achievements of the world, only to find ourselves empty and unfulfilled. I can guarantee that almost everyone reading this has some story, experience, or testimony of misguided attempts to fill the void in them. That emptiness that is often confused as loneliness. Whether you were searching for love in all the wrong places, with all the wrong people. Or trying to fill it with substances, alcohol, drugs, sex, money, cars, riches….so on and so forth. But when we turn our gaze towards God and embrace our identity in Christ, we discover a wellspring of true and lasting belonging.

Embracing our identity in Christ goes beyond mere intellectual assent or religious affiliation. It is an intimate and personal relationship with the Creator of the universe. It is the understanding that we are fearfully and wonderfully made (Psalm 139:14), intricately crafted by the hands of a loving God. It is the realization that our worth is not determined by our accomplishments, appearance, or the opinions of others, but by the immeasurable love and grace that God freely bestows upon us.

In a world that bombards us with messages of comparison, self-doubt, and unattainable standards, embracing our identity in Christ becomes a radical act of defiance. It is a declaration that we are no longer defined by the world's fleeting notions of success or beauty, but by the eternal truth that we are beloved children of God. Our worth is not measured by the number of likes on social media, the balance in our bank accounts, or the applause of others. It is rooted in the unchanging love of our Heavenly Father.

Embracing our identity in Christ also liberates us from the burden of our past mistakes, regrets, and shame. Through the redemptive work of Jesus on the cross, we are forgiven, cleansed, and made new. The chains that once bound us are broken, and we are set free to live a life of purpose and significance. No longer do we have to carry the weight of our failures or the labels that others have placed upon us. In Christ, we find restoration, healing, and the power to overcome.

When we truly embrace our identity in Christ, our lives take on new meaning and direction. The weight of trying to be perfect, to be likable goes away. We no longer strive to find our purpose in the pursuit of temporal desires or the approval of others. Instead, we seek to <u>align our hearts with God's will</u>, to discover the unique calling and purpose He has placed within us. We understand that our lives are not our own, but instruments in the hands of a loving Creator, ready to be used for His glory and the advancement of His Kingdom.

Embracing our identity in Christ empowers us to walk with confidence, knowing that we are loved, accepted, and equipped for every good work. It gives us the strength to face challenges, endure trials, and persevere in the midst of adversity. We can draw upon the limitless resources of God's grace, wisdom, and power as we navigate the complexities of life. Our identity in Christ becomes the foundation upon which we build our lives, the compass that guides our decisions, and the source of our hope and joy.

I invite you to fully embrace your identity in Christ. Take hold of the truth that you are fearfully and wonderfully made, chosen and cherished by the Creator of the universe. We don't worship the universe, as vast as it is or the things and elements in it, but the one who created it. Let go of false doctrines and false hopes. Let go of the false notions of worth and success that the world offers, and instead, anchor yourself in the unchanging love and acceptance of God. As you do, you will experience a profound transformation—a transformation that will shape every aspect of your life and enable you to live with purpose, passion, and unwavering confidence.

May you embark on this journey of embracing your identity in Christ with an open heart and a willingness to surrender to His love and grace. As you delve deeper into the truth of who you are in Him, may you discover a newfound sense of purpose, freedom, and joy. And may you become a radiant reflection of His love and goodness in the world.

Remember, you are loved, chosen, and uniquely created for a purpose. Embrace your identity in

Christ and step into the abundant life that He has prepared for you.

OVERCOMING SOCIETAL PRESSURES:

Societal pressures constantly bombard us, telling us that our worth is determined by our appearance, accomplishments, or popularity. The pursuit of external validation and conformity to societal norms can lead to a never-ending cycle of dissatisfaction and anxiety. However, when we anchor our identity in Christ, we are set free from the need for approval from others. We no longer have to conform to the world's standards because our worth is already secured in God's love.

In today's fast-paced and image-driven society, it is easy to succumb to the pressures and expectations placed upon us. Everywhere we turn, we are bombarded with messages that tell us how we should look, what we should achieve, and who we should aspire to be. The world's definition of success often revolves around external factors such as beauty, wealth, and status, leaving many feeling inadequate and constantly striving for validation.

But as followers of Christ, we are called to a different standard. Our identity is not rooted in the ever-changing opinions and standards of the world, but in the unchanging truth of God's love and acceptance. When we anchor our identity in Christ, we find liberation from the relentless pursuit of external validation and the need to conform to societal norms.

Embracing our identity in Christ means recognizing that our worth is not determined by our appearance, accomplishments, or popularity. It means understanding that we are fearfully and wonderfully made, created in the image of God Himself (Psalm 139:14). Our worth is not based on fleeting physical beauty or worldly achievements, but on the fact that we are deeply loved and valued by our Heavenly Father.

When we anchor our identity in Christ, we no longer have to conform to the world's standards of success and perfection. We can embrace our unique qualities, talents, and passions, knowing that they have been purposefully given to us by God. We are free to express ourselves authentically, without the fear of judgment or rejection. We can prioritize inner growth, character development, and the pursuit of God's will above society's expectations.

Overcoming societal pressures also means finding our worth and validation in God's love alone. We no longer need to seek affirmation from others or compare ourselves to their standards. Instead, we can rest in the truth that we are deeply loved, accepted, and cherished by our Heavenly Father. We can find our value in being children of God, knowing that our worth is not determined by our external achievements or the opinions of others.

Embracing our identity in Christ empowers us to live with authenticity, confidence, and purpose. We can resist the pressures to conform and instead focus on cultivating a character that reflects the love and grace of our Savior. We can prioritize our spiritual growth, investing in relationships, and serving others, knowing that our worth is not based on what we can do, but on who we are in Christ.

As you navigate the challenges of societal pressures, remember that your identity is rooted in Christ. You are <u>fearfully and wonderfully made</u>, and your worth is not defined by the ever-changing standards of the world. Embrace the freedom that comes from anchoring your identity in God's love and acceptance. Trust in His plan for your life and seek His guidance in all that you do.

By embracing your identity in Christ, you will discover a profound sense of purpose, fulfillment, and peace. You will find the strength to overcome the pressures of the world and live a life that is aligned with God's will. Embrace who you are in Him, and let His love be the guiding force in your life.

FINDING TRUE WORTH IN GOD:

Embracing our identity in Christ allows us to discover our true worth in God. Our worth is not contingent upon our achievements or the opinions of others. We are valuable simply because we are created in the image of God (Genesis 1:27). God's love for us is unconditional and unwavering, regardless of our performance or societal status. Understanding this truth enables us to find a deep sense of worth, purpose, and fulfillment that surpasses the fleeting measures of worldly success.

In a world that often measures worth by external factors, it is easy to fall into the trap of seeking validation and finding our value in the temporary and superficial. We may strive to meet societal expectations, chase after accolades, or compare ourselves to others, hoping that these external markers will bring us a sense of worth and fulfillment. We have all done this at some point in our lives whether we knew it or not. However, this pursuit is an endless and exhausting cycle, leaving us feeling empty and unfulfilled.

But when we embrace our identity in Christ, we discover a different source of worth—one that is unchanging and rooted in the love of our Heavenly Father. Our true worth is not found in our accomplishments, appearance, or possessions. It is found in the fact that we are deeply loved and valued by God, who created us with intention and purpose.

Understanding our worth in God's eyes allows us to release the need for approval from others and the constant striving to prove ourselves. We no longer have to measure our value by the standards of the world, because we know that our worth is already secured by the love and grace of our Heavenly Father. We are chosen, accepted, and cherished as His beloved children.

In God's eyes, we are worth more than we can comprehend. He sees the beauty and potential within us, even when we struggle to see it in ourselves. He knows every detail of our lives, and He delights in us. Our worth is not determined by our successes or failures, but by the fact that we are fearfully and wonderfully made by our Creator.

When we anchor our worth in God, we find a deep sense of security and peace. We no longer need to prove ourselves or seek validation from others, because we have already been validated by the One who matters most. This liberates us to live authentically and confidently, embracing our unique qualities, gifts, and passions.

Finding true worth in God also allows us to align our lives with His purpose for us. When we understand our inherent value, we can pursue a life that is focused on honoring Him and making a difference in the world. Our worth is not self-centered or self-serving but empowers us to love and serve others. We can use our gifts and talents to bring glory to God and impact the lives of those around us.

Your true worth is found in God, who loves you unconditionally and sees your infinite value. Embrace the truth that you are fearfully and wonderfully made, and let it transform your perspective on worth and purpose.

Let go of the need for external validation and find solace in the unchanging love of our Heavenly Father. Seek His guidance and direction as you step into the fullness of your true identity. Trust in His plan for your life, knowing that He has created you with purpose and has equipped you with everything you need to fulfill it.

THE FREEDOM TO BE AUTHENTIC:

When we embrace our identity in Christ, we are liberated to be our authentic selves. We no longer need to strive to fit into society's molds or compare ourselves to others. Instead, we can embrace our unique strengths, talents, and calling, knowing that God has a specific purpose for each of us (Ephesians 2:10). We are free to live out our true identities without the fear of judgment or rejection because our worth is rooted in God's unchanging love.

Embracing our identity in Christ grants us the freedom to be authentically ourselves. We no longer need to wear masks or hide behind a facade.

When we recognize our identity in Christ, we understand that God has uniquely designed us with specific strengths, talents, and passions. We are not meant to be carbon copies of others, but rather, we are called to shine as the individuals God created us to be. We can embrace our quirks, our unique perspectives, and our diverse gifts, knowing that they are all part of God's intentional design. We are set apart from the world and should remain that way. Not to say you cannot be involved with those outside of the body of Christ but to say that we are to be a light or example to those still searching or have yet to realize the Love of God. So do not be ashamed if you are peculiar or different form others. God makes no mistakes.

This freedom to be authentic is liberating. We no longer need to compare ourselves to others, for we understand that our worth and value come from our relationship with God, not from external measures. We are not in competition with those around us, but rather, we are called to collaborate and celebrate the unique contributions each person brings to the world.

Embracing our authentic selves also allows us to experience deeper connections with others. When we are genuine and transparent about our struggles, victories, and growth, we invite others to do the same. We create a space where vulnerability is welcomed, and relationships can flourish in an atmosphere of acceptance and love.

Additionally, our authenticity can inspire and encourage those around us. We become beacons of hope, showing others that they too can find freedom in embracing their unique selves. Our authenticity becomes a testimony to the goodness of God and the beauty of His design.

However, embracing authenticity does not mean that we have arrived at a state of perfection. We are all works in progress, continually growing and learning. There may be times when we stumble or face challenges that cause us to question our true selves. Yet, even in those moments, we can find comfort and strength in our identity in Christ.

In Him, we have the assurance that we are loved, accepted, and forgiven. We have the freedom to learn from our mistakes, to grow through challenges, and to lean on God's grace. Our identity in Christ is not dependent on our performance or our ability to be flawless, but rather, it is rooted in God's unchanging love and His transformative work in our lives.

As we embrace our authenticity, let us remember to seek God's guidance and wisdom. He is the one who knows us intimately and can reveal more to us as we journey with Him. Through prayer, meditation on His Word, and seeking wise counsel, we can gain deeper insights into our identity and purpose.

Embracing our identity in Christ is of utmost importance in a world that constantly tries to define our worth. By understanding the significance of our identity in Him, we can overcome societal pressures and find true worth in God. When we anchor our worth in His love, we experience liberation from the need for external validation and conformity. We are free to be authentic and embrace the unique purpose and calling God has placed upon our lives. Let us hold fast to our identity in Christ and live confidently in the truth that we are deeply loved, cherished, and valued by our Heavenly Father.

I invite you to step into the freedom of authenticity. Celebrate the strengths and talents He has bestowed upon you, and trust that He has a purpose for your life that is intricately woven into the tapestry of His greater plan.

May you find joy and fulfillment in being authentically you, reflecting God's love and grace to the world. May your journey of self-discovery and embracing your true identity be marked by a deep sense of freedom, peace, and purpose. And may you continually find strength in knowing that your identity in Christ is secure and unshakable.

CHAPTER 2

UNCOVERING THE LIES: CHALLENGING FALSE BELIEFS ABOUT SELF-WORTH

In our pursuit of self-worth, we often find ourselves entangled in a web of lies and misconceptions. Society bombards us with unrealistic standards, comparison traps, and a constant need for perfection. These falsehoods hinder our ability to recognize and embrace our inherent worth. In this article, we will uncover the lies that hinder self-worth by identifying common misconceptions and examining the damaging impact of comparison, perfectionism, and insecurity. By challenging these false beliefs, we can reclaim our true worth and live authentically.

IDENTIFYING COMMON MISCONCEPTIONS AND LIES:

To challenge false beliefs about self-worth, we must first identify the lies that have taken root in our minds. Some common misconceptions include:

Worth based on external factors: Society often tells us that our worth is determined by our appearance, achievements, or social status. However, this external validation is fleeting and unreliable. True self-worth transcends these superficial measures and is grounded in our inherent value as human beings.

Comparison as a measure of worth: The culture of comparison breeds insecurity and diminishes our sense of self-worth. Comparing ourselves to others robs us of joy and contentment, as we are constantly striving to meet unattainable standards. Our worth should not be defined by how we measure up to others but by embracing our unique qualities and God-given purpose.

Perfection as the ultimate goal: The pursuit of perfection is a relentless cycle that leaves us feeling inadequate and unworthy. Believing the lie that we must be flawless in every aspect of our lives hinders our self-worth. Embracing our imperfections and understanding that growth comes through learning from mistakes allows us to experience true personal growth and acceptance.

EXAMINING THE IMPACT OF COMPARISON, PERFECTIONISM, AND INSECURITY:

These three factors—comparison, perfectionism, and insecurity—significantly impact our self-worth and well-being.

Comparison: Comparing ourselves to others fuels feelings of inadequacy and undermines our self-esteem. The constant need to measure up to unrealistic standards creates a never-ending cycle of discontentment. Instead, we should focus on self-improvement, celebrating our own progress and unique journey.

Perfectionism: The pursuit of perfection sets unattainable expectations that can lead to chronic stress, anxiety, and self-doubt. It hinders our ability to appreciate our efforts and accomplishments. Embracing a mindset of growth and self-compassion allows us to cultivate a healthier sense of self-worth.

Insecurity: Insecurity stems from a lack of self-acceptance and self-belief. It robs us of the confidence to embrace our true selves and pursue our passions wholeheartedly. Recognizing and challenging the root causes of insecurity is essential for reclaiming our self-worth and living authentically.

CHALLENGING THE LIES AND CULTIVATING TRUE SELF-WORTH:

To challenge these false beliefs and cultivate true self-worth, we must take intentional steps:

Practicing self-compassion: Embracing self-compassion involves treating ourselves with kindness, understanding, and acceptance. By extending grace to ourselves and acknowledging our inherent worth, we can break free from the chains of self-criticism.

Embracing our uniqueness: Celebrating our unique qualities and strengths allows us to appreciate our individuality. Recognizing that we have a valuable contribution to make in the world cultivates a sense of purpose and enhances our self-worth.

Shifting perspectives: Instead of seeking validation from external sources, we can shift our focus inward and cultivate self-validation. Recognizing that our worth comes from God and is not dependent on others' opinions liberates us from the bondage of seeking approval and people pleasing.

Surrounding ourselves with positive influences:
Surrounding ourselves with supportive and uplifting individuals who value us for who we are helps to counteract the negative impact of comparison and insecurity. Building a network of genuine connections nurtures our self-esteem and fosters an environment of growth and acceptance.

Challenging false beliefs about self-worth is a transformative journey that requires intentional effort and self-reflection. By identifying common misconceptions and examining the impact of comparison, perfectionism, and insecurity, we can break free from the lies that hinder our self-worth.

Embracing self-compassion, celebrating our uniqueness, shifting perspectives, and surrounding ourselves with positive influences empower us to cultivate true self-worth and live authentically.

CHAPTER 3

EMBRACING GOD'S LOVE: DISCOVERING THE DEPTH OF HIS UNCONDITIONAL LOVE

God's love is the foundation upon which our lives are built. It is a love that surpasses human understanding, extending beyond our shortcomings and insecurities. In this chapter, we will explore the nature of God's love and its transformative power. We will also delve into how His love can heal our past wounds and help us develop a healthy self-image. By embracing God's love, we open ourselves to a life of healing, restoration, and unshakable identity.

EXPLORING THE NATURE OF GOD'S LOVE:

Unconditional and Unchanging: God's love for us is not based on our performance or worthiness. It is a love that remains steadfast and unwavering, even when we fall short. Understanding the unconditional nature of His love frees us from the need to earn His acceptance and affirms our inherent value. Remember, God loves you.

Sacrificial and Redemptive: God's love was demonstrated through the sacrificial act of sending His Son, Jesus Christ, to die for our sins. His love brings redemption, forgiveness, and the opportunity for new beginnings. It is a love that seeks to restore and reconcile us to Himself.

Personal and Intimate: God's love is not distant or impersonal. It is a deeply personal and intimate love that seeks to know us intimately. He knows us by name, understands our innermost thoughts and desires, and desires to have a relationship with us.

HEALING PAST WOUNDS THROUGH GOD'S LOVE:

Recognizing and Acknowledging Wounds: God's love provides a safe space for us to recognize and acknowledge the wounds we carry from our past. Through His unconditional love, we can confront the pain, trauma, and brokenness that have shaped our self-image. It is through this recognition that the healing process can begin. So, take it to God. Every trauma, every hurt, every wound.

Finding Comfort and Restoration: God's love has the power to heal our deepest wounds. As we surrender our pain to Him, He offers comfort, peace, and restoration. Through prayer, seeking His presence, and opening our hearts to His healing touch, we can experience His transformative love in our lives. Pray and allow God to teach you how to severe it from your life and allow Him to heal you.

Developing a Healthy Self-Image: God's love helps us develop a healthy self-image rooted in His truth instead of our own. Instead of defining ourselves by our past failures, insecurities, or society's standards, we can find our identity in being cherished and loved by our Heavenly Father. His love redefines our worth, reminding us that we are fearfully and wonderfully made (Psalm 139:14).

EMBRACING THE TRANSFORMATIVE POWER OF GOD'S LOVE:

Embracing Forgiveness and Grace: God's love offers forgiveness and grace, enabling us to let go of guilt, shame, and self-condemnation. Through His love, we can find freedom from the burden of our past mistakes and embrace a new identity as forgiven and redeemed children of God.

Renewing the Mind: God's love transforms our thinking patterns. As we immerse ourselves in His Word, we discover His truth and promises that counter the lies and negative self-perceptions. By aligning our thoughts with His truth, we can develop a healthy self-image and experience transformation from the inside out.

Cultivating a Relationship with God: Embracing God's love involves cultivating an intimate relationship with Him. Through prayer, worship, and spending time in His presence, we deepen our understanding of His love and experience its transformative power in our lives. This relationship provides a solid foundation for our self-worth and identity.

Embracing God's love is a life-altering journey of discovering the depth of His unconditional love. As we explore the nature of His love and its transformative power, we open ourselves to healing from past wounds and develop a healthy self-image rooted in His truth. By embracing His love, we experience freedom, restoration, and a profound sense of identity as beloved children of God. Let us immerse ourselves in the embrace of His love and allow it to shape every aspect of our lives.

CHAPTER 4

HEALING PAST WOUNDS AND DEVELOPING A HEALTHY SELF-IMAGE THROUGH GOD'S LOVE

GOD'S DESIGN: UNIQUELY CREATED FOR A PURPOSE

Recognizing that Each We is Fearfully and Wonderfully Made:

In the journey of healing past wounds and developing a healthy self-image, it is essential for people, especially women to recognize that they are fearfully and wonderfully made by God. Each man and woman is intricately designed with unique qualities, strengths, and beauty. By embracing this truth, women can begin to appreciate and celebrate their individuality, breaking free from the societal pressures to conform to certain standards or expectations.

Discovering and Embracing Personal Gifts, Talents, and Passions:

As we embark on the path of self-discovery, we can explore and embrace our personal gifts, talents, and passions. God has endowed each person with specific abilities and interests, uniquely positioning them to make a difference in the world. By identifying and nurturing these gifts, we can find fulfillment and purpose, aligning our self-image with our God-given identity.

HEALING PAST WOUNDS AND DEVELOPING A HEALTHY SELF-IMAGE

Embracing God's Healing Love

To heal past wounds, women must first open their hearts to embrace God's healing love. Through prayer, reflection, and surrendering their pain to Him, they can experience the transformative power of His love. God's love brings comfort, restoration, and healing to the broken places within, allowing women to move forward with a renewed sense of self-worth and purpose.

Embracing Forgiveness and Letting Go of the Past

Forgiveness is a vital aspect of healing and developing a healthy self-image. By recognizing that God's love offers forgiveness for our past mistakes, people can release the burden of guilt and shame. Letting go of the past allows them to embrace the truth of their forgiven and redeemed identity in Christ, freeing them to live in the present and future with confidence.

Renewing the Mind and Embracing God's Truth

Healing and developing a healthy self-image require a renewal of the mind through embracing God's truth. Men and Women can immerse themselves in His Word, meditating on His promises and affirmations of love, worth, and purpose. By aligning their thoughts with His truth, they can overcome negative self-perceptions, insecurities, and limiting beliefs, embracing a positive self-image rooted in God's perspective.

Seeking Support and Community

Healing and developing a healthy self-image are not journeys meant to be undertaken alone. Men and Women can seek support from trusted mentors, counselors, or support groups within their Christian community. Surrounding themselves with individuals who can provide guidance, encouragement, and accountability creates an environment conducive to growth, healing, and the development of a healthy self-image.

Healing past wounds and developing a healthy self-image are integral parts of our journey towards embracing our identity in Christ. All of us carry wounds from our past experiences—painful memories, traumas, or negative beliefs about ourselves—that can hinder our ability to see ourselves as God sees us. However, through God's love and grace, we can experience profound healing and restoration.

Recognizing and acknowledging these past wounds is an important first step. Often, we may have buried these hurts deep within us, trying to move forward without addressing the pain they have caused. But in order to heal, we must bring them into the light and allow God to work in those areas of brokenness.

In the process of healing, it is crucial to remember that our identity is not defined by our past. Our worth and value are not determined by the wounds we carry, but by the redemptive work of Christ on the cross. God sees us as His beloved children, beautifully and wonderfully made, regardless of our past experiences.

As we surrender our pain to God, we invite Him to bring healing and restoration into our lives. This may involve seeking professional support such as counseling or therapy, where we can process our emotions and gain valuable insights into our past wounds. It may also involve engaging in practices like prayer, meditation, and journaling, allowing God's presence to bring comfort and healing to our hearts.

In the journey of healing, it is important to extend ourselves grace and forgiveness. This includes forgiving others who may have caused us pain and forgiving ourselves for any mistakes or regrets we may hold onto. Forgiveness does not excuse the actions or diminish the pain, but it frees us from the burden of carrying resentment and bitterness. It opens the door for God's healing to flow into our lives.

Developing a healthy self-image goes hand in hand with healing. As we embrace our identity in Christ, we learn to see ourselves through

God's eyes. We understand that we are fearfully and wonderfully made, created in His image with unique gifts, talents, and purpose. Our value is not determined by our physical appearance, accomplishments, or the opinions of others. It is rooted in the unconditional love and acceptance of our Heavenly Father.

Cultivating a healthy self-image involves renewing our minds with the truth of God's Word. We immerse ourselves in Scriptures that affirm our identity in Christ and remind us of our worth. We meditate on passages that speak of God's love, grace, and purpose for our lives. By aligning our thoughts with God's truth, we can break free from the negative self-perceptions that have held us captive.

Additionally, surrounding ourselves with a supportive Christian community is essential in developing a healthy self-image. We need people who will encourage, uplift, and speak truth into our lives. They can serve as reminders of God's love and help us see ourselves through His eyes when our own vision becomes clouded. Together, we can journey towards healing, growing, and embracing our true identities in Christ.

Dear reader, I encourage you to embark on the transformative path of healing and developing a healthy self-image. Embrace the truth that your past does not define you, and that God's love has the power to bring restoration to every area of your life. Seek His guidance and surround yourself with a community of believers who will walk alongside you in this journey.

Remember, healing takes time, and it is a process unique to each individual. Be patient with yourself, and trust that God is at work in you. As you open your heart to His healing touch, may you experience the freedom, joy, and wholeness that comes from embracing your true identity in Christ.

Healing past wounds and developing a healthy self-image through God's love is a transformative process that involves recognizing our unique design, embracing personal gifts and passions, and receiving His healing and forgiveness. Through His love and the renewal of the mind, we can experience healing, restoration, and the freedom to live authentically. Let each man and woman embrace their unique identity in Christ and confidently step into their God-given purpose. It is a journey that requires openness, vulnerability, and a willingness to surrender to God's plan.

In seeking God's will for our lives, we acknowledge that He has a specific purpose and calling for each one of us. It is not about conforming to societal expectations or pursuing worldly success, but about aligning our hearts with His desires and surrendering our plans to His perfect guidance. As we seek His will through prayer, scripture, and discernment, we open ourselves to the transformative power of His leading.

Stepping into our true identity through God requires a deep understanding of His love for us. It is through His love that we find the strength to overcome obstacles, let go of self-doubt and fear, and embrace the fullness of who He created us to be. We can find confidence and assurance in knowing that we are beloved children of God, chosen and cherished by Him.

Practical exercises can aid us in this transformative process. Journaling our thoughts and prayers, reflecting on our passions and talents, and seeking guidance from trusted mentors and spiritual leaders can help us gain clarity and discern God's direction. Reading and meditating on biblical teachings that affirm our identity in Christ can strengthen our faith and reshape our perspective.

As we journey towards living a purposeful life aligned with God's plan, it is important to remember that His timing is perfect. We may encounter seasons of waiting, challenges, or unexpected detours along the way. However, in those moments, we can trust that God is working all things together for our good (Romans 8:28). He is shaping and molding us, preparing us for the fulfilling and impactful purpose He has in store.

Embrace your identity in God. It may require courage and stepping out of your comfort zone but know that you are not alone. God walks beside you every step of the way, guiding, comforting, and empowering you.

As you discover your unique design, embrace your personal gifts and passions, and receive God's healing and forgiveness, you will find a renewed sense of self-worth and purpose. Remember that your worth is not determined by the opinions of others or the standards of this world, but by the immeasurable love of your Heavenly Father.

CHAPTER 5

GOD'S DESIGN: UNIQUELY CREATED FOR A PURPOSE

Every person is fearfully and wonderfully made by God, intricately designed with a purpose and unique qualities. In this chapter, we will explore the significance of recognizing our individuality and embracing God's design for our lives. And this chapter is centered around women but men can take this chapter and apply it as well.

RECOGNIZING THAT EACH WOMAN IS FEARFULLY AND WONDERFULLY MADE:

God's creation is a masterpiece, and each woman is a precious part of that masterpiece.

By recognizing this truth, we can begin to appreciate our inherent worth and value. It is essential to understand that our worth is not determined by external standards or societal expectations but is rooted in the truth that we are fearfully and wonderfully made by a loving Creator.

Embracing Physical and Inner Beauty: God's design extends beyond our physical appearance. It encompasses our inner qualities, such as kindness, compassion, wisdom, and strength. Embracing both our physical and inner beauty allows us to cultivate a healthy self-image and appreciate the unique attributes that make us who we are.

Emphasizing Identity over Comparison: Recognizing our unique design helps us shift our focus from comparison to embracing our own identity. Each woman has been given a specific purpose and set of qualities that make her irreplaceable. Instead of striving to be like others, we can celebrate our individuality and contribute our unique gifts to the world. By understanding that our identity is rooted in God's love and purpose for us, we can break free from the destructive cycle of comparison. Comparing ourselves to others only leads to feelings of inadequacy, envy, and discontentment. Instead, we can find contentment and joy in embracing who we are and the unique path that God has set before us.

It is essential to remember our worth is not determined by how we measure up to others. When we shift our focus from comparison to embracing our own identity, we allow ourselves to fully express and develop the gifts that God has entrusted to us.

Furthermore, embracing our identity over comparison opens the door for collaboration and support rather than competition. When we recognize the value in our unique design, we can celebrate and appreciate the diverse gifts and talents of others. Instead of feeling threatened by their success, we can cheer them on and learn from them. Together, we can contribute to a harmonious community that reflects the beautiful diversity of God's creation.

PRACTICAL EXERCISES

Practical exercises can help us shift our mindset from comparison to embracing our identity. One powerful exercise is to create a gratitude journal where we daily write down the qualities, strengths, and accomplishments that make us who we are. Reflecting on these positive aspects helps us appreciate our own journey and the unique contributions we bring.

As Christians, avoiding comparison and embracing our identity in God requires a shift in our perspective and intentional steps towards aligning our thoughts and actions with biblical principles. Here are some practical steps to help you in this process:

1. **Ground Yourself in God's Word:**
Regularly study and meditate on the Word of God. Scripture provides us with the truth about who we are in Christ and the unchanging nature of God's love for us. By immersing ourselves in God's Word, we gain a solid foundation and a proper understanding of our identity as His children.

2. **Focus on God's Approval:** Seek to please God above seeking the approval of others. Remember that our worth is not determined by what others think of us but by our relationship with God. Strive to live in a way that honors Him and brings glory to His name, rather than trying to meet societal expectations or gain validation from others.

3. **Practice Gratitude:** Cultivate an attitude of gratitude by regularly reflecting on the blessings and gifts that God has bestowed upon you. Gratitude shifts our focus from what we lack to what we have, helping us appreciate our unique journey and the blessings that come with it.

4. **Celebrate Others**: Instead of comparing yourself to others, learn to celebrate and genuinely rejoice in the successes and

strengths of others. Recognize that their achievements do not diminish your own worth or identity. By embracing a mindset of encouragement and celebration, you contribute to a community that uplifts and supports one another.

5. **Guard Your Thoughts:** Be mindful of the thoughts that enter your mind and actively combat negative self-talk or comparisons. When comparison thoughts arise, intentionally replace them with affirmations of your identity in Christ and the truth of God's love for you. Capture those thoughts and make them obedient to Christ (2 Corinthians 10:5).

6. **Serve Others:** Shift your focus from self-centered comparison to selfless service. Engage in acts of kindness and love towards others, using your unique gifts and talents to

bless those around you. When we serve others, we experience the joy of making a positive impact rather than dwelling on our own perceived shortcomings.

7. **Surround Yourself with Positive Influences:** Choose your company wisely. Surround yourself with like-minded individuals who support and encourage you in your faith journey. Engage in Christian communities, small groups, or mentoring relationships where you can find encouragement, accountability, and affirmation in your identity in Christ.

8. **Seek God's Guidance:** Regularly seek God's guidance through prayer. Surrender your desires, dreams, and insecurities to Him, and ask Him to guide you in embracing your identity and purpose in Him. Trust in His

leading and timing, knowing that He has a unique plan for your life.

Remember, embracing your identity in God is a lifelong journey that requires constant renewal of the mind and intentional effort. It is not about striving for perfection but about growing in your understanding of who God created you to be. By aligning your thoughts, actions, and attitudes with God's truth, you can avoid the trap of comparison and confidently embrace your unique identity in Him.

Additionally, spending intentional time in prayer and meditation allows us to connect with God, who lovingly affirms our identity and purpose. Seeking His guidance and asking Him to reveal His plan for our lives helps us gain clarity and confidence in embracing our individuality.

Here are some scriptures that reinforce the importance of avoiding comparison and embracing our identity in God. *These can be used in prayer.*

1. Galatians 6:4-5 - "Each one should test their own actions. Then they can take pride in themselves alone, without comparing themselves to someone else, for each one should carry their own load."

2. Psalm 139:14 - "I praise you because I am fearfully and wonderfully made; your works are wonderful; I know that full well."

3. 1 Corinthians 12:4-6 - "There are different kinds of gifts, but the same Spirit distributes them. There are different kinds of service, but the same Lord. There are different kinds of

working, but in all of them and in everyone it is the same God at work."

4. Romans 12:2 - "Do not conform to the pattern of this world, but be transformed by the renewing of your mind. Then you will be able to test and approve what God's will is—his good, pleasing and perfect will."

5. 2 Corinthians 10:12 - "We do not dare to classify or compare ourselves with some who commend themselves. When they measure themselves by themselves and compare themselves with themselves, they are not wise."

6. Ephesians 2:10 - "For we are God's handiwork, created in Christ Jesus to do good works, which God prepared in advance for us to do."

7. Psalm 46:10 - "Be still, and know that I am God."

8. Colossians 3:12 - "Therefore, as God's chosen people, holy and dearly loved, clothe yourselves with compassion, kindness, humility, gentleness, and patience."

These scriptures remind us of our unique value and purpose in God's eyes, the dangers of comparison, and the importance of embracing our individual gifts and calling. Meditating on these verses can help reinforce our identity in Christ and guide us in avoiding comparison as we strive to live out our God-given purpose. As we prioritize our identity in Christ and focus on embracing who we are, we become empowered to live authentically and make a meaningful impact in the world. Our unique gifts and talents are not meant to be hidden but to be shared for the glory of God and the betterment of others.

So, let us choose to celebrate our individuality and resist the temptation of comparison. Remember that your worth and purpose extend far beyond what the world may dictate. Embrace who you are, cultivate your strengths, and confidently step into the purpose that God has prepared for you. The world is waiting for the unique contribution that only you can bring.

DISCOVERING AND EMBRACING PERSONAL GIFTS, TALENTS, AND PASSIONS:

God has equipped each of us with specific gifts, talents, and passions to fulfill our purpose in life. Discovering and embracing these attributes empowers us to live with intentionality and impact. Here are some steps to guide us in this journey:

Self-Reflection and Assessment: Take time to reflect on your interests, strengths, and talents. Consider the activities that bring you joy and fulfillment. Reflect on the moments when you feel most alive and engaged. Through self-assessment, you can gain insight into your unique gifts and passions.

Seeking God's Guidance: Invite God into the process of discovering your purpose. Pray for wisdom, discernment, and clarity. Seek His guidance through His Word and listen to the promptings of the Holy Spirit. Trust that God will reveal the path He has designed specifically for you. If you don't know what all your gifts are, ASK GOD.

Exploring New Opportunities: Step out of your comfort zone and explore new opportunities that align with your interests and passions. Engage in activities, classes, or projects that allow you to develop and express your unique gifts. Be open to new experiences and be willing to learn and grow along the way.

Embracing Growth and Development: Embracing your personal gifts and talents involves continuous growth and development. Seek opportunities for further learning and honing your skills. Surround yourself with mentors, role models, and supportive communities that can help you cultivate your gifts and encourage you on your journey.

Discovering and embracing our personal gifts, talents, and passions allows us to live a life of purpose and fulfillment. Let us celebrate the beauty of our uniqueness and trust in God's design for our lives as we embrace the journey of self-discovery and impact the world with our God-given gifts.

CHAPTER 6

FINDING PURPOSE: SEEKING GOD'S WILL FOR YOUR LIFE

Discovering our purpose is a lifelong journey that requires seeking God's guidance and surrendering to His timing. In this chapter, we will explore the process of seeking God's will for our lives and understanding that purpose unfolds in seasons. By engaging in prayer, immersing ourselves in Scripture, and practicing discernment, we can align our lives with God's purpose and experience a deep sense of fulfillment and meaning.

SEEKING GUIDANCE THROUGH PRAYER, SCRIPTURE, AND DISCERNMENT:

Prayer

Prayer is a powerful tool for seeking God's guidance. Through heartfelt and intentional prayer, we can commune with God, expressing our desires, concerns, and questions. As we quiet our hearts and listen for His voice, we open ourselves to receive His wisdom and direction.

Scripture

The Bible is a rich source of divine wisdom and guidance. Regularly immersing ourselves in Scripture helps us understand God's character, His promises, and the principles that shape our lives. By studying God's Word, we gain insights into His will and discern His purpose for our lives.

Discernment

Discernment involves seeking the Holy Spirit's guidance in making decisions and understanding God's will. It requires attentiveness to His leading, a willingness to surrender our desires, and the ability to distinguish between God's voice and other influences. Practicing discernment helps us align our choices with God's purpose and direction.

Here are some scriptures that emphasize the importance of seeking and finding purpose in God:

1. Proverbs 16:9 - "In their hearts humans plan their course, but the Lord establishes their steps."

2. Jeremiah 29:11 - "For I know the plans I have for you," declares the Lord, "plans to prosper you and not to harm you, plans to give you hope and a future."

3. Ephesians 2:10 - "For we are God's handiwork, created in Christ Jesus to do good works, which God prepared in advance for us to do."

4. Psalm 37:4 - "Take delight in the Lord, and he will give you the desires of your heart."

5. Romans 12:2 - "Do not conform to the pattern of this world, but be transformed by the renewing of your mind. Then you will be able to test and approve what God's will is—his good, pleasing and perfect will."

6. Proverbs 3:5-6 - "Trust in the Lord with all your heart and lean not on your own understanding; in all your ways submit to him, and he will make your paths straight."

7. Matthew 6:33 - "But seek first his kingdom and his righteousness, and all these things will be given to you as well."

8. Colossians 3:23-24 - "Whatever you do, work at it with all your heart, as working for the Lord, not for human masters, since you know that you will receive an inheritance from the Lord as a reward. It is the Lord Christ you are serving."

These scriptures remind us that God has a purpose and plan for each of us. By seeking Him, trusting in His guidance, and aligning our hearts with His will, we can discover and fulfill our unique calling in life. Reflecting on these verses and seeking God's direction through prayer and meditation can help us find clarity and direction in pursuing our purpose in Him.

UNDERSTANDING THAT PURPOSE UNFOLDS IN SEASONS:

Embracing God's Timing

Recognizing that purpose unfolds in seasons requires embracing God's timing. We live in a world that often emphasizes instant gratification and achievement, but God's plan unfolds according to His perfect timing. Trusting in His sovereignty and having patience allow us to surrender our timelines and embrace the seasons of preparation, growth, and waiting.

Finding Purpose in the Present

Purpose is not solely tied to future accomplishments or specific roles. It is also found in the present moment, in faithfully living out our daily lives for God's glory. Embracing the tasks, relationships, and opportunities before us with a heart of service and gratitude allows us to find purpose in every season.

Navigating Transitions

Life is marked by various transitions, and each transition presents an opportunity for growth and redirection. During times of change, we can seek God's guidance and trust that He is leading us into a new season of purpose. Even in uncertain times, His faithfulness remains constant, and He can use transitions to shape us and align us with His plans.

Finding purpose is a continuous journey of seeking God's will and embracing His timing. Through prayer, Scripture, and discernment, we can align our lives with His purpose and experience a deep sense of fulfillment. Understanding that purpose unfolds in seasons allows us to trust God's plan, find purpose in the present, and navigate transitions with confidence. As we walk in step with God, seeking His guidance and surrendering to His timing, we embark on a life that is deeply meaningful and aligned with His divine purpose for us.

CHAPTER 7

OVERCOMING OBSTACLES: NAVIGATING CHALLENGES TO YOUR IDENTITY

In our journey of embracing our identity in Christ, we will inevitably face obstacles that challenge our self-worth and purpose. In this chapter, we will address common obstacles such as self-doubt, fear, and failure. We will explore strategies for overcoming these challenges and developing resilience and faith in God's plan during difficult times. By equipping ourselves with the tools to navigate these obstacles, we can emerge stronger, more confident, and steadfast in our identity in Christ.

ADDRESSING COMMON OBSTACLES: SELF-DOUBT, FEAR, AND FAILURE

Self-Doubt

Self-doubt can undermine our confidence and hinder us from fully embracing our identity in Christ. We will explore the roots of self-doubt, such as comparison and negative self-talk, and learn strategies to combat it. Through prayer, affirming God's truth, and surrounding ourselves with supportive communities, we can overcome self-doubt and walk in the assurance of our worth and purpose.

Self-doubt can be a relentless voice that whispers lies about our worth and capabilities. It stems from comparing ourselves to others, societal pressures, past failures, and negative self-talk. However, as followers of Christ, we have the assurance that our worth is not determined by our own efforts or the opinions of others. Our identity is firmly rooted in God's love and grace.

To overcome self-doubt, we must first recognize its presence in our lives. We need to identify the triggers and thought patterns that contribute to our self-doubt. Are we constantly comparing ourselves to others on social media? Are we allowing the negative voices in our heads to drown out God's truth? By becoming aware of these patterns, we can begin to challenge and replace them with God's perspective.

Prayer becomes our refuge in moments of self-doubt. We can bring our fears, insecurities, and doubts before God, pouring out our hearts to Him. As we seek His presence and guidance, we open ourselves up to receiving His truth and affirmation. Through prayer, we invite God to transform our thoughts and align them with His truth.

Affirming God's truth is another powerful tool in combating self-doubt. We can immerse ourselves in Scripture, meditating on verses that remind us of our identity in Christ. Verses like Psalm 139:14, which says, "I praise you because I am fearfully and wonderfully made; your works are wonderful, I know that full well," affirm our inherent worth as God's creation. By intentionally replacing self-doubting thoughts with God's truth, we can silence the voice of self-doubt and embrace the truth of our identity in Christ.

Surrounding ourselves with a supportive Christian community is crucial in overcoming self-doubt. We need people who will speak life and encouragement into our lives, reminding us of our value and potential. In community, we find accountability, prayer support, and mentorship that can help us navigate through seasons of self-doubt. Together, we can celebrate victories, offer grace in setbacks, and grow in our understanding of who we are in Christ.

Fear

Fear can paralyze us and keep us from stepping into God's calling for our lives. We will identify common fears, such as the fear of failure, rejection, or inadequacy, and examine how they impact our identity. By entrusting our fears to God, renewing our minds with His promises, and taking courageous steps of faith, we can conquer fear and walk in the fullness of our identity as daughters of God.

Fear is a powerful emotion that can hold us captive and prevent us from stepping into our true identity and purpose. It often arises when we face the unknown, take risks, or encounter challenges. However, as Christians, we are called to walk in faith and not be driven by fear. Fear itself is of the enemy (2 Timothy 1:7).

To overcome fear, we must surrender it to God. We can bring our fears before Him, acknowledging our limitations and asking for His strength and guidance. In times of fear, we can find comfort in knowing that God is with us, and His perfect love casts out fear (1 John 4:18). He promises to be our refuge and strength, an ever-present help in trouble (Psalm 46:1).

Trusting in God's faithfulness is essential in overcoming fear. We can remind ourselves of His past faithfulness in our lives and in the lives of others. Reflecting on how He has provided, protected, and guided us in the past strengthens our trust in Him for the future. As we lean on His promises, we can take steps forward in faith, knowing that He is faithful to fulfill His plans for us.

Stepping out of our comfort zone is often necessary to grow and fulfill our purpose. While fear may try to hold us back, we can choose to embrace courage. With God as our source of strength, we can take bold steps, knowing that He goes before us and equips us for every task. We can lean on His power and rely on His guidance, trusting that He will enable us to overcome our fears and accomplish His purposes in our lives.

Failure

Failure is an inevitable part of life, but it does not define our worth or purpose. We will shift our perspective on failure, recognizing it as an opportunity for growth, learning, and God's redirection. By embracing a growth mindset, seeking God's wisdom in our failures, and finding strength in His grace, we can overcome the fear of failure and persevere in our pursuit of God's plan for our lives.

Failure is an inevitable part of life. It can leave us feeling discouraged, questioning our abilities, and doubting our worth. However, as Christians, we can view failure through a different lens. Failure does not define us; it is an opportunity for growth and learning.

In moments of failure, it is crucial to remind ourselves that our worth is not tied to our achievements or successes. Our worth is grounded in God's unconditional love and acceptance of us. When we experience failure, we can turn to God, seeking His forgiveness and guidance. He is always ready to extend His grace and help us learn from our mistakes.

Scripture reminds us that God's strength is made perfect in our weakness (2 Corinthians 12:9). In our moments of failure, we can surrender our pride, acknowledge our need for God's strength, and allow Him to work in and through us. Failure becomes an opportunity to rely on His power, develop resilience, and grow in our faith.

Developing a healthy perspective on failure involves embracing a growth mindset. Instead of viewing failure as the end, we can approach it as a stepping stone toward progress. We can reflect on the lessons learned, make necessary adjustments, and press forward with renewed determination. God can use our failures to shape us, refine our character, and redirect our paths toward His purposes.

In addressing the common obstacles of self-doubt, fear, and failure, we are called to rely on God's truth and promises. Through prayer, affirming His truth, seeking support from a Christian community, surrendering our fears, and embracing a growth mindset, we can navigate these obstacles with confidence. As we overcome these hurdles, we step into the fullness of our identity in Christ, embracing our worth, purpose, and the abundant life He has called us to live.

DEVELOPING RESILIENCE AND FAITH IN GOD'S PLAN DURING DIFFICULT TIMES

Cultivating Resilience

Resilience is the ability to bounce back from adversity. We will explore practical strategies for developing resilience, such as nurturing a strong support system, practicing self-care, and seeking professional help when needed. By leaning on God's strength, we can weather difficult seasons and emerge stronger, knowing that He works all things together for our good.

Faith plays a central role in developing resilience. Trusting in God's plan and His faithfulness, even when circumstances are challenging, can anchor us during difficult times. We can draw strength from Scripture, meditating on verses that remind us of God's presence, provision, and sovereignty. Verses like Romans 8:28 affirm that God works all things together for the good of those who love Him, even in the midst of trials.

Seeking God's perspective and surrendering our circumstances to Him can also cultivate resilience. Through prayer, we can lay our burdens before Him, acknowledging our limitations and entrusting our lives into His loving hands. As we surrender control and trust in His wisdom, we find peace and the assurance that He is working behind the scenes, even when we cannot see the bigger picture.

It is important to acknowledge that there may be times when professional help is needed to navigate difficult seasons. Seeking the guidance of a trusted counselor or therapist can provide valuable tools and perspectives to navigate through challenging emotions, trauma, or mental health struggles. God can work through these professionals to bring healing, clarity, and renewed resilience to our lives.

In developing resilience, it is crucial to remember that it is a journey. It is not about being immune to pain or never experiencing hardships. Rather, it is about learning to trust God's faithfulness, leaning on Him for strength, and growing in our ability to bounce back from adversity. As we cultivate resilience, we become equipped to face future challenges with courage and a deepened faith in God's plan for our lives.

By embracing these strategies and relying on God's strength, we can develop resilience and navigate difficult times with hope and perseverance. As we anchor ourselves in God's promises, we can emerge from trials stronger, wiser, and more resilient, knowing that He is faithful and will guide us through every season of life.

Trusting God's Plan

During challenging times, it can be tempting to question God's plan and lose sight of our identity in Him. We will explore the importance of trusting God's sovereignty, even when His plan seems unclear or different from our expectations. By surrendering our desires and trusting in His faithfulness, we can find peace, hope, and purpose amidst life's trials.

One important aspect of trusting God's plan is surrendering our desires and expectations. As humans, we often have our own ideas and plans for how our lives should unfold. We may have dreams and goals that we believe will lead to fulfillment and happiness. However, when our plans are not aligned with God's will, we can experience disappointment and confusion.

In these moments, it is essential to remind ourselves that God's ways are higher than our ways (Isaiah 55:9). He sees the bigger picture, and His plans are rooted in His infinite wisdom and love for us. It requires humility and a willingness to let go of our own agenda and trust that His plan is ultimately for our good.

Trusting God's plan also means finding peace in His faithfulness. Throughout Scripture, we see countless examples of God's faithfulness to His people. He has a track record of fulfilling His promises and working all things together for the good of those who love Him (Romans 8:28). Reflecting on His faithfulness in our own lives and the testimonies of others can strengthen our trust in His plan, even when we cannot fully comprehend it.

It is important to remember that trusting God's plan does not mean that life will be free from challenges or hardships. In fact, we are told in Scripture that we will face trials of various kinds (James 1:2-4). However, our trust in God allows us to navigate these trials with hope and assurance that He is with us every step of the way.

Trusting God's plan requires us to walk by faith and not by sight (2 Corinthians 5:7). It means relinquishing control and embracing the unknown, knowing that God is faithful to guide us and provide for us. It is a daily surrender, where we lay our desires, fears, and doubts at His feet, and choose to trust Him wholeheartedly.

As we trust God's plan, we can find peace, hope, and purpose. We can rest in the assurance that He is working behind the scenes, orchestrating every detail of our lives. Even in the midst of uncertainty, we can have confidence that His plan is perfect and that He will use our circumstances for His glory and our ultimate good.

Trusting God's plan does not mean we passively wait for things to happen. It involves actively seeking His guidance through prayer, studying His Word, and seeking wise counsel from fellow believers. It requires us to align our hearts and minds with His truth and to be open to His leading, even when it takes us outside our comfort zones.

In the process of trusting God's plan, we may discover that His plan for our lives is even greater and more fulfilling than we could have ever imagined. It may involve unexpected detours, challenges, and moments of stretching and growth. However, through it all, we can find purpose and joy as we walk in obedience to Him.

Trusting God's plan is a lifelong journey, and there may be moments when doubts arise or when we struggle to understand His ways. In those moments, it is important to draw closer to Him, to seek His presence and wisdom, and to allow His peace to guard our hearts and minds (Philippians 4:6-7).

Learn from past experiences. Reflecting on past challenges and how God has been faithful in bringing us through them can give us confidence and reassurance for the present difficulties. Remembering His faithfulness in the past can help us trust Him in the present and future.

Surrender to God's timing. It is natural to desire quick solutions and immediate relief from our struggles. However, developing resilience involves surrendering to God's timing and trusting that He knows what is best for us. It may require patience and perseverance as we wait for His plans to unfold.

Remember that developing resilience is a process that takes time and intentional effort. It is a journey of growth and transformation, and God is with us every step of the way. As we rely on His strength and trust in His plan, we will find that our faith deepens, our resilience strengthens, and our perspective align with His eternal purposes.

Seeking God's Guidance

In the midst of obstacles and challenges, seeking God's guidance is essential. We must acknowledge that we cannot navigate life's complexities on our own. Our Heavenly Father is eager to provide us with wisdom, direction, and discernment as we journey toward embracing our true identity in Christ and fulfilling our purpose.

Prayer is a powerful tool that allows us to communicate with God and seek His guidance. Through prayer, we can pour out our hearts, express our fears and doubts, and seek His wisdom. It is in these moments of surrender and vulnerability that we open ourselves to hearing

His voice and receiving His guidance. As we invite God into our decisions, big or small, He will direct our paths and illuminate the way forward.

Additionally, Scripture serves as a guidebook for life. It contains timeless wisdom and truths that can inform our choices, challenge our perspectives, and provide encouragement during challenging times. By regularly immersing ourselves in God's Word, we open ourselves to divine revelation and insights that can shape our decisions and actions.

Moreover, seeking the counsel of trusted mentors and wise believers can provide valuable perspectives and guidance. God often uses godly individuals to speak truth into our lives, offer encouragement, and provide practical wisdom. Their experiences, knowledge, and discernment can help us navigate obstacles and make informed decisions. However, it is crucial to seek counsel from those who align with biblical principles and exhibit a genuine walk with God.

As we seek God's guidance, we must also cultivate a spirit of surrender and humility. Recognizing that God's ways are higher than ours and His plans are perfect, we surrender our own agendas and desires. Trusting in His goodness, we acknowledge that His guidance may not always align with our preferences or expectations. Yet, we can rest assured that His plans are far greater and more fulfilling than anything we could ever envision.

In seeking God's guidance, it is important to be patient and attentive. Sometimes His answers come swiftly, while other times we must wait and trust in His perfect timing. During periods of waiting, we can use this time to grow in faith, deepen our relationship with Him, and develop the virtues of patience and trust.

To actively seek God's guidance, consider implementing these practices:

1. Set aside dedicated time for prayer and meditation, inviting God into your decision-making process.

2. Establish a consistent habit of studying and meditating on Scripture, allowing God's Word to shape your thoughts and actions.

3. Seek out wise counsel from mentors and fellow believers who have a mature faith and can provide biblical perspectives.

4. Pay attention to the promptings of the Holy Spirit and listen for God's voice through inner peace, confirmations, or redirection.

5. Remain open and teachable, willing to adjust your plans and perspectives as God leads.

6. Be patient and trust in God's timing, knowing that His guidance is worth the wait.

By seeking God's guidance in all areas of our lives, we align ourselves with His will and purpose. We acknowledge that He is the ultimate source of wisdom and direction, and our trust in His guidance frees us from the burden of making decisions based on our limited understanding. As we walk in obedience and surrender to His leading, we can confidently embrace our true identity in Christ and step into the purpose He has prepared for us.

Let us invite God into every aspect of our lives, seeking His guidance and relying on His wisdom. With His help, we can navigate challenges, overcome obstacles, and live a purposeful life aligned with His divine plan. As we embark on this transformative journey, may we embrace our identity in Christ, trust in His guidance, and experience the abundant life He has in store for us.

Overcoming obstacles is an integral part of our journey to embrace our identity in Christ. By addressing common challenges such as self-doubt, fear, and failure, and developing resilience and faith in God's plan during difficult times, we can grow stronger and more rooted in our identity. With God's help, we can overcome these obstacles and walk in the fullness of our purpose, knowing that He is with us every step of the way. Let us face challenges with courage, trusting in God's unfailing love and His unwavering commitment to shaping us into the women He has called us to be.

CHAPTER 8

WALKING IN CONFIDENCE: STEPPING INTO YOUR TRUE IDENTITY

Walking in confidence is a transformative aspect of embracing our true identity in Christ. In this chapter, we will explore the key elements of cultivating a healthy self-esteem grounded in Christ's love and embracing God's promises to live boldly for His glory. By understanding our worth in Him and aligning our lives with His purpose, we can walk in confidence, radiate His love, and fulfill our God-given potential.

CULTIVATING A HEALTHY SELF-ESTEEM GROUNDED IN CHRIST'S LOVE:

Understanding Your Identity in Christ

Our true identity is rooted in Christ. We will dive into the biblical truths that define who we are in Him, such as being chosen, loved, forgiven, and empowered by His Spirit. By embracing these truths, we can build a strong foundation for a healthy self-esteem that is anchored in God's unwavering love for us.

Our identity in Christ is not based on the ever-changing opinions of the world or our own self-perception. Instead, it is founded on the unchanging truth of who God says we are. As we delve into the depths of this profound identity, we will uncover the biblical truths that define us as followers of Christ.

First and foremost, we are chosen. Ephesians 1:4 declares that God chose us in Christ before the foundation of the world. Before we took our first breath, God had already set His affection on us and called us into a personal relationship with Him. This truth reminds us that we are not accidents or mere products of chance, but intentional creations with a purpose.

Moreover, we are deeply loved by God. 1 John 4:10 affirms that God's love for us is not based on our performance or worthiness but on His very nature as love itself. His love is unconditional, unending, and unfathomable. When we grasp the enormity of God's love, it transforms our perspective of ourselves. We no longer need to seek validation or love from others because we are fully embraced by the love of our Heavenly Father.

In Christ, we are also forgiven. Ephesians 1:7 assures us that in Him, we have redemption and the forgiveness of sins. The weight of guilt and shame is lifted as we realize that our past mistakes and failures do not define us. Through the sacrificial death of Jesus Christ on the cross, we have been washed clean, made righteous in God's sight, and given a fresh start. This truth enables us to let go of self-condemnation and embrace the freedom and joy of living in God's grace.

Furthermore, as believers, we are empowered by the Holy Spirit. Acts 1:8 reminds us that we have received the indwelling presence of the Holy Spirit, who empowers us to live victoriously and fulfill God's purpose for our lives. The same Spirit that raised Jesus from the dead dwells within us, equipping us with spiritual gifts, wisdom, and strength to navigate life's challenges and make a difference in the world.

Understanding these foundational truths about our identity in Christ lays the groundwork for a healthy self-esteem that is not rooted in our accomplishments, appearance, or the opinions of others. Instead, it is anchored in the unchanging love and acceptance of our Heavenly Father. This realization liberates us from the need for external validation and empowers us to live authentically, confident in who we are as beloved children of God.

By embracing our identity in Christ, we can overcome the lies of the enemy, the pressures of society, and the insecurities within ourselves. We can walk in the freedom and confidence that come from knowing we are chosen, loved, forgiven, and empowered by God. This understanding shapes our self-image, influences our decisions, and enables us to live purposefully for His glory.

As we journey on the path of understanding our identity in Christ, let us immerse ourselves in the riches of God's Word, allow His truth to permeate our hearts, and walk confidently in the knowledge that we are chosen, loved, forgiven, and empowered by our Heavenly Father. May this profound understanding of our identity fuel us to live purposefully, passionately, and joyfully as we fulfill God's plan for our lives.

Overcoming Negative Self-Talk

Negative self-talk is a common struggle that many of us face. It is the internal dialogue of negative thoughts, self-criticism, and self-doubt that can undermine our confidence and hinder us from fully embracing our true identity in

Christ. However, we can overcome negative self-talk by implementing practical strategies that empower us to challenge and replace those negative thoughts with God's truth.

Renewing our minds with God's Word is a foundational step in overcoming negative self-talk. The Bible is filled with promises, affirmations, and truths that remind us of our worth and identity in Christ. By regularly immersing ourselves in Scripture, we can counteract negative thoughts with the truth of God's Word. For example, when we find ourselves thinking, "I'm not good enough," we can counteract that thought with the truth that we are fearfully and wonderfully made (Psalm 139:14) and that God's grace is sufficient for us (2 Corinthians 12:9).

Affirming God's promises is another powerful tool in combatting negative self-talk. When we intentionally speak affirmations based on God's truth, we shift our focus from self-doubt to the assurance of His love and faithfulness. By regularly affirming statements such as "I am chosen and loved by God" (1 Peter 2:9), "I am more than a conqueror through Christ" (Romans 8:37), and "I can do all things through Christ who strengthens me" (Philippians 4:13), we embed these truths deep within our hearts and minds.

In addition to renewing our minds with God's Word and affirming His promises, it is crucial to be aware of the source of negative self-talk. Often, negative thoughts are rooted in comparison, past failures, or distorted perceptions of ourselves. By recognizing these triggers, we can challenge the validity of these thoughts and replace them with the truth. We can ask ourselves questions like, "Is this thought based on reality or my own insecurities?" or "What does God say about me in His Word?" This intentional self-reflection allows us to separate fact from fiction and align our thoughts with God's truth.

Surrounding ourselves with a supportive Christian community is also essential in overcoming negative self-talk. We need people who will speak truth into our lives, encourage us, and remind us of our identity in Christ. Engaging in small group Bible studies, joining a mentoring program, or seeking accountability from trusted friends can provide us with the encouragement and support we need to combat negative self-talk. Being in community allows us to share our struggles, receive prayer, and grow together as we seek to align our thoughts with God's truth.

Lastly, prayer is a powerful weapon in overcoming negative self-talk. Through prayer, we invite God into our thought processes and ask Him to transform our minds. We can pour out our insecurities, doubts, and fears before Him, knowing that He cares for us (1 Peter 5:7). As we surrender our thoughts to Him, we open ourselves up to His guidance, healing, and transformation. Prayer enables us to replace negative self-talk with God's truth and experience the peace and confidence that come from aligning our minds with His will. Prayer silences every negative voice in your mind.

Overcoming negative self-talk is an ongoing journey that requires intentionality, persistence, and reliance on God's strength. It is not a quick fix, but a gradual process of transformation. As we consistently apply these strategies, we will witness a shift in our self-perception, a greater sense of confidence, and a deeper understanding of our true identity in Christ. Remember, God's truth has the power to dispel lies, break chains, and renew our minds. Let us actively challenge and replace negative self-talk with the empowering truth of God's Word, embracing our identity and walking in the freedom and confidence that come from knowing who we are in Him.

Practicing Self-Compassion and Self-Care

In our journey of embracing our identity in Christ, it is crucial to cultivate self-compassion and prioritize self-care. Often, we can be harsh critics of ourselves, holding ourselves to unrealistic standards and dwelling on our imperfections. However, when we extend grace and compassion to ourselves, we align our perspective with God's love and acceptance.

Self-compassion is about treating ourselves with kindness, understanding, and forgiveness, just as God extends His grace and mercy to us. It involves acknowledging that we are not perfect and that making mistakes is a part of being human. Instead of berating ourselves for our shortcomings, self-compassion encourages us to offer ourselves empathy and understanding.

Embracing our imperfections is a crucial aspect of self-compassion. We live in a world that often emphasizes perfection and highlights our flaws and failures. However, as children of God, we are reminded that we are fearfully and wonderfully made (Psalm 139:14). Embracing our imperfections means recognizing that our worth is not based on our performance or outward appearance but on our inherent value as God's beloved creations.

In addition to self-compassion, self-care plays a vital role in nurturing our self-esteem and well-being. Self-care involves intentionally prioritizing activities and practices that nourish our minds, bodies, and spirits. It is about recognizing our worth and investing in ourselves, not as an act of selfishness but as an act of stewardship of the lives God has given us.

Self-care can take various forms, depending on our individual needs and preferences. It may involve setting boundaries and saying no to activities or relationships that drain us emotionally and mentally. It may include engaging in activities that bring us joy, such as hobbies, exercise, spending time in nature, or engaging in creative pursuits. It may also involve seeking support and counseling when needed, as well as taking time for rest, relaxation, and rejuvenation.

By practicing self-compassion and self-care, we demonstrate a deep understanding of our identity as fearfully and wonderfully made by God. We recognize that we are worthy of love, care, and nourishment. As we prioritize self-compassion and self-care, we are better equipped to navigate challenges, bounce back from setbacks, and maintain a healthy self-esteem rooted in God's love.

Furthermore, when we practice self-compassion and self-care, we model a healthy and balanced approach to life for others. Our example can inspire and encourage those around us to also embrace their identity in Christ and prioritize their well-being. It is through nurturing ourselves that we can better serve and love others, fulfilling our purpose to be a light in the world.

In conclusion, practicing self-compassion and self-care is essential for nurturing a healthy self-esteem and embracing our identity in Christ. By extending grace to ourselves, embracing our imperfections, and prioritizing self-care practices, we align our perspective with God's truth about who we are. As we cultivate self-compassion and self-care, we grow in our understanding of our inherent worth as beloved children of God and are empowered to live purposeful and fulfilling lives for His glory.

EMBRACING GOD'S PROMISES AND LIVING BOLDLY FOR HIS GLORY:

Anchoring in God's Promises

In our journey of embracing our identity in Christ, anchoring ourselves in God's promises is of utmost importance. His promises are like solid anchors that provide us with strength, assurance, and hope, especially during times of fear and uncertainty.

Throughout the Scriptures, we find numerous promises that God has made to His people. These promises encompass various aspects of our lives, including provision, guidance, protection, and empowerment. When we anchor our faith in these promises, we can overcome doubt, insecurity, and the challenges that come our way.

God promises to provide for our needs, assuring us that He will never leave us lacking (Philippians 4:19). He promises to guide us, offering His wisdom and direction when we seek Him with all our hearts (Proverbs 3:5-6). In times of danger and adversity, He promises to be our refuge and stronghold, protecting us from harm (Psalm 91:1-2). Furthermore, He promises to equip us with His Holy Spirit, empowering us to fulfill the purposes He has ordained for our lives (Acts 1:8).

By anchoring our faith in God's promises, we find strength to face the challenges and uncertainties that come our way. His promises serve as a firm foundation on which we can stand, knowing that He is faithful to fulfill His word. They remind us that we are not alone in our journey, but rather, we have a loving and powerful God who walks beside us every step of the way.

When we hold onto God's promises, we can move forward with confidence, even in the face of adversity. We can trust that His plans for our lives are good, and He will bring them to fruition (Jeremiah 29:11). His promises give us hope and assurance, reminding us that He is in control and working all things together for our ultimate good (Romans 8:28).

As we immerse ourselves in His Word, meditating on His promises, we are reminded of His faithfulness throughout history and in our own lives. We can find comfort, encouragement, and strength in the realization that the same God who made these promises is with us today, steadfast and unwavering.

Anchoring ourselves in God's promises is an essential aspect of embracing our identity in Christ. His promises provide us with the strength, assurance, and hope we need to navigate through life's challenges. By placing our trust in His word, we can overcome fear and uncertainty, knowing that He is faithful to fulfill all that He has promised. Let us hold onto His promises, allowing them to anchor us in His love, grace, and purpose for our lives.

Stepping Out in Faith

Living boldly for God's glory often requires us to step out of our comfort zones and embrace opportunities for growth and impact. It means taking courageous steps of faith, even when faced with uncertainty or opposition.

When God calls us to something, He equips us for the task. We can trust in His strength and guidance as we step out in faith. It may not always be easy, and we may encounter obstacles along the way, but with God by our side, we can overcome any challenge.

Stepping out in faith requires us to let go of our own limitations and trust in God's limitless power. It means surrendering our fears, doubts, and insecurities, and placing our confidence in His promises. We can be assured that He will never leave us nor forsake us.

Living boldly for God's glory means embracing His calling on our lives and pursuing it wholeheartedly. It means using our unique gifts, talents, and passions to make a difference in the world around us. It means being willing to take risks and embrace new opportunities, knowing that God is with us every step of the way.

As we step out in faith, we become vessels for God's work. We become instruments of His love, grace, and mercy. Our lives become a testimony to His faithfulness and transformative power. Through our boldness, we can inspire and impact others, pointing them towards the hope and salvation found in Christ.

So, let us step out in faith, trusting in God's provision and guidance. Let us embrace the opportunities He presents, even if they seem daunting. With Him leading the way, we can live boldly for His glory, knowing that He has a purpose and plan for our lives. May our steps of faith be a testament to His greatness and a catalyst for His kingdom to come on earth as it is in heaven.

Radiating God's Love and Truth

Confidence in Christ empowers us to radiate His love and truth to the world. When we fully embrace our identity as children of God, we become vessels through which His character shines forth. Our words, actions, and interactions with others become opportunities to reflect His love and truth.

To radiate God's love, we must first receive it ourselves. We can immerse ourselves in His Word, seeking to understand and experience the depth of His love for us. As we receive His love, it naturally overflows to those around us. We can show kindness, compassion, and forgiveness, reflecting the love that God has poured into our hearts.

Radiating God's truth involves aligning our lives with His Word. It means speaking the truth in love, even when it may be uncomfortable or unpopular. We can live with integrity, honoring God's principles and standing firm on His truth, regardless of the prevailing cultural norms. By living authentically and consistently with His truth, we become beacons of light in a world often clouded by deception and darkness.

Practical ways to radiate God's love and truth include acts of service, extending grace to others, and engaging in meaningful conversations that point people towards God. By being intentional in our relationships and interactions, we can create spaces where others feel valued, heard, and loved.

As we radiate God's love and truth, we become ambassadors of His kingdom. Our lives become living testimonies of His transformative power and the hope found in Christ. Through our confident expression of His love and truth, we have the opportunity to impact lives, bring healing to brokenness, and draw others closer to God.

Let us embrace our identity in Christ and boldly radiate His love and truth. May our lives be a reflection of His character, illuminating the path for others to encounter His love, experience His truth, and find eternal purpose and fulfillment.

Walking in confidence is a transformative journey that involves cultivating a healthy self-esteem grounded in Christ's love and embracing God's promises to live boldly for His glory. By understanding our identity in Him, challenging negative self-talk, and practicing self-compassion, we build a solid foundation for confidence. By anchoring ourselves in God's promises and stepping out in faith, we can embrace His calling and impact the world around us. May we walk in the confidence that comes from knowing we are loved and chosen by Him, and may our lives radiate His love and truth for His glory and the benefit of others.

CHAPTER 9

LIVING A PURPOSEFUL LIFE: IMPACTING OTHERS FOR GOD'S KINGDOM

Living a purposeful life goes beyond personal fulfillment; it is about making a meaningful impact on others and advancing God's Kingdom. In this chapter, we will explore how our unique purpose aligns with God's Kingdom work and discover practical ways to serve, inspire, and influence others through our identity in Christ. By embracing our role in God's plan and intentionally engaging in acts of service and influence, we can live a purposeful life that leaves a lasting legacy.

DISCOVERING HOW OUR UNIQUE PURPOSE ALIGNS WITH GOD'S KINGDOM WORK:

Uncovering Your God-Given Gifts and Passions

Within each of us lies a treasure trove of God-given gifts, talents, and passions waiting to be discovered and unleashed. These unique attributes are not random or accidental but purposefully woven into the very fabric of our being. They are divine clues that lead us to our God-ordained purpose.

During our journey, we will embark on practical exercises to uncover and understand these gifts and passions. We will explore our strengths, skills, and interests, seeking patterns and connections that reveal our true calling. Through self-reflection, prayer, and seeking wise counsel, we will gain clarity on the areas where we excel and find deep joy.

It is essential to recognize that our gifts and passions are not meant for self-gratification alone but for God's Kingdom work. As we align our unique attributes with His purposes, we discover a profound sense of fulfillment and impact. Our gifts become tools in His hands, enabling us to serve others, build up the body of Christ, and make a meaningful difference in the world.

In the process of uncovering our gifts and passions, we may encounter challenges and doubts. We may question our abilities or compare ourselves to others. However, we must remember that God equips and empowers us for the tasks He calls us to. Our worth and significance do not stem from comparison or external validation but from our identity in Christ.

As we step into the discovery and utilization of our gifts and passions, let us do so with humility and a willingness to surrender to God's guidance. Let us embrace the uniqueness of our design and celebrate the diversity of the body of Christ. Together, we can create a beautiful tapestry of service, each playing our part and impacting the world for His glory.

Uncovering our God-given gifts and passions is a lifelong journey. It requires ongoing self-reflection, growth, and openness to God's leading. As we commit ourselves to this process, we unlock the fullness of our potential and align ourselves with God's purpose for our lives. Let us embark on this adventure, confident that as we step into our God-given gifts and passions, we will find fulfillment, joy, and the ability to impact the world in ways we never imagined.

Seeking God's Direction

In our pursuit of purpose, seeking God's direction is not only beneficial but essential. It is through His guidance that we can discern the path He has prepared for us and align our purpose with His divine plan. This requires humility, surrender, and a willingness to lay down our own desires and plans before Him.

Through prayer, we open the channels of communication with our Heavenly Father. We express our desires, concerns, and uncertainties, inviting Him to speak to our hearts and reveal His will. In the stillness of His presence, we find clarity and direction, as He gently guides us along the path, He has ordained for us.

Reflection is another vital component of seeking God's direction. It involves introspection, examining our motives, and evaluating the alignment of our desires with His Word. As we reflect on our strengths, passions, and opportunities, we invite the Holy Spirit to illuminate our understanding and reveal His plans for our lives.

Discernment is a gift from God that allows us to distinguish His voice from the noise of the world. It is a spiritual practice that involves attuning our hearts to the promptings of the Holy Spirit and filtering our decisions through the lens of God's Word. As we develop a deeper relationship with Him, our discernment becomes sharper, and we can more confidently navigate the choices and challenges that come our way.

Seeking God's direction is not a one-time event but an ongoing process. It requires an active pursuit of His will in every aspect of our lives. It means surrendering our desires, dreams, and plans, trusting that His ways are higher, and His thoughts are greater than ours.

By aligning our purpose with God's will, we ensure that our efforts are focused on what truly matters. We become instruments in His hands, vessels through which His love, grace, and truth can flow into the world. Our purpose becomes intertwined with His Kingdom agenda, and our lives take on a greater significance as we participate in His redemptive work.

As we seek God's direction, let us remember that His plans are always good, perfect, and pleasing (Romans 12:2). We can trust that He knows what is best for us and that He will guide us along the path of purpose. May our hearts be open, our spirits attentive, and our steps aligned with His divine leading. In doing so, we will experience the joy and fulfillment that come from living a purposeful life in harmony with God's will.

Embracing Opportunities for Growth and Learning

Living a purposeful life is not a stagnant journey but a continuous process of growth and learning. It requires a willingness to step out of our comfort zones and embrace new experiences, challenges, and opportunities for personal development. As we do so, we expand our impact and deepen our understanding of how our unique purpose intersects with God's Kingdom work.

Embracing opportunities for growth and learning opens doors to new perspectives, skills, and insights. It pushes us beyond our limitations and stretches our capabilities. When we step out of our comfort zones, we discover hidden strengths and untapped potential that we may not have been aware of before. It is in these moments of stretching and growth that we uncover new aspects of our purpose and develop a greater sense of self-awareness.

Challenges and new experiences provide fertile ground for personal development. They allow us to develop resilience, perseverance, and problem-solving skills. Through these experiences, we learn to rely on God's strength and wisdom, recognizing that we are not meant to navigate life's challenges in our own power but in the power of the Holy Spirit.

Embracing growth and learning also deepens our understanding of how our purpose aligns with God's Kingdom work. As we engage in new experiences and expand our horizons, we gain insights into the needs of others, the issues plaguing our world, and the areas where God is calling us to make a difference. We become more attuned to the heartbeat of God and more effective in fulfilling our unique role in advancing His Kingdom.

However, embracing growth and learning requires vulnerability and a willingness to embrace uncertainty. It means letting go of the familiar and stepping into the unknown. It may involve taking risks, facing failures, and experiencing discomfort. Yet, it is in these moments of stretching that we grow the most and discover the full extent of our God-given potential.

As we journey towards living a purposeful life, let us embrace opportunities for growth and learning. Let us be open to new experiences, challenges, and the refining process that comes with them. May we approach each opportunity with a humble heart, a teachable spirit, and a reliance on God's guidance. By doing so, we will continually expand our impact, deepen our understanding of our purpose, and walk in alignment with God's plans for our lives.

PRACTICAL WAYS TO SERVE, INSPIRE, AND INFLUENCE OTHERS THROUGH OUR IDENTITY IN CHRIST:

Serving Others with Love and Compassion

One of the most beautiful and impactful ways to live out our identity in Christ is by serving others with love and compassion. It is through selfless acts of kindness and extending a helping hand that we tangibly express God's love to those around us. As we embrace our purpose and step into our true identity, we will explore practical ways to extend love, grace, and compassion to those in need.

Serving others begins with a heart that is open and willing to see the needs of those around us. It requires a genuine desire to make a positive difference in the lives of others, regardless of their background, circumstances, or status. By cultivating a heart of compassion and empathy, we become vessels through which God's love flows to touch and transform lives.

Practical acts of kindness can take many forms. It can be as simple as offering a listening ear to someone who is going through a difficult time or lending a helping hand to a neighbor in need. It can involve volunteering our time and talents to organizations and causes that align with our values. It can mean reaching out to the marginalized and forgotten, extending love and support to those who may feel unseen or unheard.

Serving others also involves stepping out of our comfort zones and embracing the opportunity to meet the physical, emotional, and spiritual needs of those around us. It requires us to be intentional in seeking out opportunities to make a positive impact, even in the smallest of ways. By doing so, we not only bless others but also experience the joy and fulfillment that comes from selfless giving.

In our service, we are not only demonstrating God's love but also participating in His redemptive work in the world. Each act of kindness and each moment of selfless service has the power to bring transformation and hope to those who need it most. It is through our willingness to serve that we become instruments of God's grace and agents of His Kingdom on earth.

As we seek to live a purposeful life aligned with God's plan, let us be intentional in our commitment to serve others with love and compassion. May we open our hearts and extend our hands to those in need, recognizing that in serving others, we are serving Christ Himself. May our acts of kindness be a reflection of God's love and a catalyst for positive change in the lives of those we encounter.

Inspiring Others through Authenticity and Vulnerability

Our authenticity and vulnerability have the power to inspire and encourage others on their own journeys. When we share our testimonies, challenges, and victories, we allow others to see the transformative work of God in our lives. In this chapter, we will explore the importance of embracing vulnerability and opening up about our experiences, creating a safe space for others to find hope, healing, and inspiration.

Sharing our stories requires a willingness to be authentic and vulnerable. It means being honest about our struggles, doubts, and failures, as well as our moments of growth, faith, and triumph. By opening up about our own journey, we break down walls of pretense and perfectionism, creating an environment where others feel safe to be themselves and share their own experiences.

When we share our stories, we offer a glimpse into the faithfulness and goodness of God. Our vulnerabilities become bridges of connection, allowing others to relate to our humanity and find solace in the fact that they are not alone in their struggles. As we reveal the ways in which God has worked in our lives, we become living testimonies of His grace and redemption.

By embracing vulnerability, we also create opportunities for empathy and understanding. When we share our challenges and vulnerabilities, we give others permission to do the same. In this space of authenticity, we can offer support, encouragement, and prayer for one another. We find strength in our shared experiences and create a community that fosters growth and healing.

Moreover, our vulnerability allows us to be conduits of hope and inspiration. When we share our victories and moments of breakthrough, we demonstrate the power of God to transform lives. Our stories become beacons of light, guiding others on their own paths of healing and transformation. Through our authenticity, we inspire others to embrace their own unique journeys and trust in God's faithfulness.

As we navigate the chapter on inspiring others through authenticity and vulnerability, let us remember that our stories have the potential to touch hearts, ignite faith, and bring about positive change. May we have the courage to embrace vulnerability, trusting that God can use our stories to impact lives and bring glory to His name. May our authenticity create a ripple effect of inspiration, leading others to find hope and purpose in their own lives.

Influencing Others with God's Truth and Wisdom

As ambassadors of Christ, we have the incredible opportunity and responsibility to positively influence the lives of others. In this chapter, we will explore practical ways to share God's truth, wisdom, and love through our words, actions, and relationships. By living out our identity in Christ and imparting His values and principles, we can make a lasting impact on the lives of those around us.

Our influence begins with aligning our lives with the truth and wisdom found in God's Word. As we deepen our understanding of His principles and teachings, we are better equipped to reflect His character in our daily lives. This alignment involves intentional choices to live in obedience to His commands and to seek His guidance in all areas of our lives.

One of the most powerful ways to influence others is through our words. Our speech has the ability to build up, encourage, and inspire those around us. By speaking words of truth, love, and grace, we can bring light into darkness and speak life into the hearts of others. Whether through gentle guidance, heartfelt encouragement, or timely wisdom, our words can make a significant impact on those who hear them.

However, our influence goes beyond mere words. It is also manifested through our actions and the way we live our lives. When we demonstrate integrity, kindness, compassion, and forgiveness in our interactions with others, we exemplify the transformative power of God's love. Our actions become a tangible expression of His truth and wisdom, drawing others closer to Him.

In addition to our words and actions, our relationships play a vital role in influencing others. By cultivating authentic connections and investing in the lives of those around us, we create opportunities to share God's truth and wisdom in a personal and meaningful way. Through our genuine care, support, and guidance, we can help others navigate challenges, grow in their faith, and discover their own purpose in Christ.

Let us remember that our influence is not about forcing our beliefs on others, but rather about living out our faith in a way that inspires and invites others to experience the transformative power of God's love. May we approach this privilege with humility, grace, and sensitivity, allowing the Holy Spirit to guide our words and actions. May our influence be marked by genuine love and a desire to see others thrive in their relationship with God.

Living a purposeful life is not solely about personal achievements but about impacting others for God's Kingdom. By discovering how our unique purpose aligns with God's Kingdom work and engaging in practical ways to serve, inspire, and influence others through our identity in Christ, we can live a life that leaves a lasting legacy. Let us embrace our role in God's plan, seek His guidance, and actively engage in acts of service and influence. May our lives reflect the love, grace, and truth of Jesus Christ, and may our actions bring glory to God and draw others closer to Him.

Living a Purpose-Filled Life:

Embracing our identity in Christ unlocks the door to living a purpose-filled life. It is a transformative journey that shapes our perspective, motivates our actions, and infuses our entire existence with meaning and significance. When we fully grasp the truth of our identity as children of God, co-heirs with Christ, and vessels of His love and grace, we experience a profound shift in how we approach life.

Confidence and Boldness:

Knowing our identity in Christ empowers us with a newfound confidence and boldness. We understand that we are not mere spectators or passive participants in the world but active agents of change. We have the assurance that God has equipped us with everything we need to fulfill the purpose He has for us. With this knowledge, we step forward with boldness, knowing that we are backed by the power of the Holy Spirit and guided by God's wisdom.

As children of God, we are secure in His love, and our confidence stems from our identity rooted in Him. We can overcome self-doubt, fear, and insecurities, knowing that we are unconditionally loved and accepted by our Heavenly Father. This confidence empowers us to take risks, step out of our comfort zones, and embrace opportunities to make a meaningful impact.

Sense of Purpose:

Our identity in Christ also ignites within us a deep sense of purpose. We recognize that we are not here by chance or accident, but that God has uniquely designed and called us for a specific purpose. We are part of a grand narrative of His redemptive plan, and our lives play a significant role in His Kingdom work.

With this understanding, our actions, choices, and relationships take on a new dimension of meaning. We no longer wander aimlessly, driven by worldly pursuits or the need for approval. Instead, we are driven by a desire to glorify God in everything we do. Our purpose becomes intertwined with the fulfillment of His will and the advancement of His Kingdom on Earth.

Making a Difference:

Living a purpose-filled life means making a tangible difference in the lives of others. As vessels of God's love and grace, we are called to extend His compassion, kindness, and mercy to those around us. Our identity in Christ compels us to love sacrificially, serve selflessly, and share the good news of salvation with a hurting world.

We become channels of God's love, shining His light in the darkest corners and bringing hope to the hopeless. Whether it is through acts of kindness, speaking words of encouragement, sharing our faith, or using our talents and resources to meet the needs of others, we understand that our purpose is intricately connected to impacting lives for His glory.

Living a purpose-filled life also involves seeking justice, fighting for the oppressed, and standing up for truth and righteousness. As ambassadors of Christ, we are called to be salt and light in the world, actively participating in God's mission to bring transformation and restoration.

Embracing our identity in Christ is the catalyst for living a purpose-filled life. It enables us to approach life with confidence, boldness, and a deep sense of purpose. We understand that we are children of God, co-heirs with Christ, and vessels of His love and grace. Our actions, choices, and relationships are infused with meaning as we seek to glorify God and make a difference in the lives of others.

Let us embrace our identity in Christ wholeheartedly and allow it to shape every aspect of our lives. May we live with a confident assurance of who we are and the purpose for which we are called. And as we journey on, let us continually seek God's guidance and the leading of the Holy Spirit, as we actively participate in His redemptive work and make an impact for His Kingdom.

CHAPTER 10

SUSTAINING YOUR IDENTITY: NURTURING A LIFELONG JOURNEY

Embracing our identity in Christ is not a one-time event but a lifelong journey. In this chapter, we will explore the importance of sustaining and nurturing our identity in Christ. We will discuss the significance of cultivating daily habits and spiritual disciplines that help us maintain a strong identity in Christ. Additionally, we will emphasize the value of surrounding ourselves with a supportive Christian community that encourages and uplifts us in our journey of faith.

CULTIVATING DAILY HABITS AND SPIRITUAL DISCIPLINES:

Cultivating daily habits and spiritual disciplines is essential for nurturing our relationship with God and strengthening our identity in Christ. In this chapter, we will explore the importance of consistent practices such as prayer, meditation, Bible study, and worship. These habits not only deepen our understanding of God's Word but also help us align our thoughts, desires, and actions with His will.

Through prayer, we open up a direct line of communication with God, allowing us to express our joys, concerns, and desires while also listening for His guidance and wisdom. By setting aside dedicated time each day for prayer, we develop a deeper intimacy with our Heavenly Father.

Meditation on Scripture allows us to dwell on God's truth, internalize His promises, and apply His Word to our lives. As we immerse ourselves in the Scriptures, we gain a clearer understanding of who God is and how He wants us to live.

Bible study is a transformative practice that enables us to explore the depths of God's Word, gaining insights, wisdom, and revelation. By engaging with Scripture through various study methods, we uncover profound truths that shape our perspective, inform our decisions, and mold our character.

Worship is an expression of our love, adoration, and reverence for God. It lifts our spirits, renews our faith, and draws us into His presence. Whether through music, prayer, or acts of service, worship helps us cultivate a heart of gratitude and surrender, aligning our focus on God's goodness and faithfulness.

By consistently practicing these spiritual disciplines, we create a rhythm of intimacy with God that sustains and empowers us. These habits serve as a spiritual lifeline, nourishing our souls and deepening our connection with our Heavenly Father. They provide the foundation for living a purposeful life aligned with God's plan, as we continually seek His guidance, grow in His love, and walk in obedience to His Word.

Prayer and Scripture Study: Prayer is our direct line of communication with God, and studying His Word allows us to deepen our understanding of His character and His will for our lives.

Worship and Gratitude: Worshiping God and expressing gratitude are powerful ways to cultivate a heart that is aligned with our identity in Christ. By focusing our hearts on God's goodness and faithfulness, we nurture a vibrant and resilient identity in Him.

SURROUNDING YOURSELF WITH A SUPPORTIVE CHRISTIAN COMMUNITY:

Importance of Christian Fellowship: Surrounding ourselves with a supportive Christian community is crucial for sustaining our identity in Christ. The significance of fellowship, accountability, and encouragement from fellow believers who share our faith journey is important. By engaging in authentic relationships, we can find support, guidance, and affirmation in our pursuit of a Christ-centered identity.

Participating in Small Groups and Church Communities:

Small groups and church communities play a crucial role in our spiritual journey. In this chapter, we will explore the significance of actively engaging in small groups, Bible studies, and church activities that foster fellowship and discipleship. By participating in these communities, we create an environment for deeper connection, spiritual growth, and mutual support.

One of the key benefits of joining a small group or Bible study is the opportunity for deeper connection with fellow believers. In these intimate settings, we can share our joys, struggles, and questions, knowing that we are surrounded by people who are walking alongside us on the same journey. Through open and honest discussions, we learn from one another, gain new perspectives, and find encouragement and support in times of need.

Furthermore, small groups and church communities provide a space for spiritual growth. By studying the Word of God together, we deepen our understanding of His truth and learn how to apply it to our daily lives. We can ask questions, engage in meaningful discussions, and receive guidance and mentorship from more experienced believers. In this environment, we are challenged to grow in our faith, develop a closer relationship with God, and live out the teachings of Jesus Christ.

Active participation in church communities also allows us to contribute our unique gifts and talents for the benefit of others. As we serve and support one another, we create a culture of mutual edification and encouragement. We can use our God-given abilities to minister to others, whether through acts of service, leading small groups, or using our creative talents to enhance worship and outreach.

In addition to these personal benefits, participating in small groups and church communities also enables us to share our faith experiences with others. By sharing our testimonies and journeying alongside fellow believers, we can inspire and encourage one another. Our stories of God's faithfulness and transformative work in our lives become a powerful testimony to His love and grace.

As we explore the chapter on participating in small groups and church communities, let us approach these gatherings with a spirit of openness, humility, and willingness to learn and grow. May we actively engage in fellowship, invest in the lives of others, and contribute our gifts and talents for the glory of God and the building up of His Kingdom. Together, let us create a community where all members are valued, supported, and empowered to live out their purpose in Christ.

Seeking Mentors and Spiritual Guides: Mentors and spiritual guides play a significant role in our journey of sustaining our identity in Christ. Seeking wise counsel from mature believers who can provide guidance, support, and accountability. By learning from their experiences and wisdom, we can navigate challenges and grow in our identity and faith.

Sustaining our identity in Christ requires intentional effort and commitment. By cultivating daily habits and spiritual disciplines that align us with God's truth, and by surrounding ourselves with a supportive Christian community, we can nurture a lifelong journey of faith. Let us prioritize prayer, Scripture study, worship, and self-reflection to strengthen our identity in Christ. Let us also seek fellowship, engage in small groups, and find mentors who can guide and encourage us. As we sustain our identity in Christ, may we grow in our love for Him, our understanding of His purpose for our lives, and our ability to impact the world with His transformative love and grace.

CHAPTER 11

THE IMPORTANCE OF KNOWING YOUR IDENTITY IN CHRIST AND ITS IMPACT ON HEALING FROM TRAUMA AND FINDING PURPOSE

In the depths of our souls, we long for healing from the wounds of trauma, and we yearn for a sense of purpose that gives our lives meaning and direction. In this chapter, we will explore the profound significance of knowing our identity in Christ and how it impacts our ability to heal from trauma and find purpose. We will delve into the transformative power of understanding who we are in Him, how it brings healing to our wounded hearts, and how it provides a solid foundation for discovering and embracing our purpose in life.

THE IDENTITY IN CHRIST:

Knowing our identity in Christ goes beyond simply acknowledging our belief in Him. It is about understanding and embracing the truth of who we are in Him. When we accept Jesus as our Savior, we become new creations, adopted as children of God, and co-heirs with Christ. This identity forms the bedrock of our faith and sets the stage for healing and purpose in our lives.

HEALING FROM TRAUMA:

Finding Healing in God's Love
Understanding our identity in Christ helps us find healing from trauma by experiencing God's

unconditional love. The wounds of trauma can leave us feeling broken, unworthy, and unlovable. But in Christ, we discover that we are deeply loved, accepted, and cherished. His love becomes the balm that soothes our wounded hearts, bringing restoration and healing to our brokenness.

Embracing Forgiveness and Redemption

Knowing our identity in Christ enables us to embrace forgiveness and redemption, both for ourselves and for others involved in our trauma. In Him, we find the strength to forgive those who have hurt us and release the burden of bitterness and resentment. We also recognize that we are forgiven and free from the guilt and shame that often accompany trauma. This newfound freedom paves the way for emotional and spiritual healing.

Embracing Our True Worth and Value

Trauma can strip away our sense of worth and value, leaving us feeling insignificant and powerless. However, knowing our identity in Christ reveals our true worth and value. We understand that we are fearfully and wonderfully made, created with a purpose and destined for greatness. This understanding empowers us to reclaim our self-worth and embrace a positive self-image.

FINDING PURPOSE:

Discovering God's Plan for Our Lives

Knowing our identity in Christ is the key to discovering our purpose. We recognize that we are not accidents or products of random chance but intentional creations with a unique purpose. God has a plan for each one of us, and by understanding our identity in Christ, we open ourselves up to His guidance and direction. He reveals our purpose step by step, leading us on a journey of fulfillment and impact.

Aligning Our Gifts and Passions

Our identity in Christ helps us align our gifts, talents, and passions with God's plan for our lives. As we grow in our understanding of who we are in Him, we become more attuned to the desires and abilities He has placed within us. We discover that our gifts and passions are not accidental but intentional components of our purpose. By aligning them with His Kingdom work, we find fulfillment and make a significant impact.

LIVING A PURPOSE-FILLED LIFE:

Embracing our identity in Christ enables us to live a purpose-filled life. When we fully grasp our identity as children of God, co-heirs with Christ, and vessels of His love and grace, we approach life with confidence, boldness, and a sense of purpose. Our actions, choices, and relationships are infused with meaning as we seek to glorify God and make a difference in the lives of others.

Knowing our identity in Christ is not a mere intellectual understanding but a transformative experience that shapes our entire being. It brings healing to our wounded hearts, liberates us from the chains of trauma, and propels us toward our God-given purpose. As we anchor ourselves in the truth of who we are in Him, we find solace, restoration, and empowerment. We become agents of healing and hope in a broken world, guided by our identity in Christ and driven by our purpose. May we never underestimate the importance of knowing our identity in Christ, for it holds the key to our healing and the fulfillment of our purpose.

THE IDENTITY IN CHRIST:

Knowing our identity in Christ is a transformative journey that goes beyond surface-level beliefs. It encompasses a deep understanding and wholehearted embrace of the truth of who we are in Him. When we accept Jesus as our Savior, we are not just forgiven and saved; we are fundamentally changed at the core of our being.

As new creations in Christ, we are reborn spiritually. Our old self, marked by sin and brokenness, is crucified with Him, and we rise to a new life infused with His righteousness and grace. This profound transformation shapes our identity and sets us apart from the world.

One crucial aspect of our identity in Christ is being adopted as children of God. Through His boundless love, we are welcomed into His family, no longer outsiders but beloved sons and daughters. We are embraced by His unconditional love, accepted in our imperfections, and bestowed with the inheritance of His Kingdom.

Additionally, our identity in Christ extends to being co-heirs with Christ. We share in His glory, His victory over sin and death, and His eternal purpose. As co-heirs, we have a divine destiny, intimately connected to the redemptive work of Christ. This inheritance is not just a future promise, but a present reality that impacts every aspect of our lives.

Understanding and embracing this identity in Christ is vital because it forms the bedrock of our faith. It shapes our worldview, influences our decisions, and provides a firm foundation for our healing and purpose. When we truly grasp the truth of who we are in Him, it transforms how we perceive ourselves, others, and the world around us.

In the context of healing, knowing our identity in Christ brings profound restoration to our wounded hearts. Trauma can leave us feeling shattered, lost, and disconnected from our sense of self. But when we anchor ourselves in the truth of our identity in Christ, we find solace and healing.

Understanding that we are children of God assures us of His unconditional love and constant presence. In the depths of our pain, we can find comfort knowing that we are not alone but embraced by the arms of our Heavenly Father. His love becomes the healing balm that soothes our wounds, restores our brokenness, and brings wholeness to our shattered souls.

Additionally, our identity in Christ enables us to find purpose amidst our pain. It assures us that our suffering is not in vain, but can be transformed into a testimony of His redeeming power. Through our experiences of healing and restoration, we become vessels of His grace and agents of compassion to others who are hurting.

By embracing our identity in Christ, we are empowered to live purposefully. It ignites a passion within us to fulfill the calling and destiny that God has placed on our lives. We realize that our purpose is not based on societal expectations, achievements, or external validation, but on aligning our lives with His divine plan.

Our identity in Christ helps us discover our unique gifts, talents, and passions, which are woven into the fabric of our purpose. It motivates us to use these gifts to impact the world, shining His light and extending His love to those around us. Whether it's serving, teaching, creating, leading, or comforting, we recognize that our purpose is intricately connected to the greater story of God's Kingdom.

In conclusion, knowing our identity in Christ is a transformative journey that shapes every aspect of our lives. It is the foundation upon which our healing from trauma and our discovery of purpose are built. As we embrace our identity as new creations, adopted children of God, and co-heirs with Christ, we find healing, purpose, and an unwavering assurance of His love. May we continually deepen our understanding and embrace of our identity in Christ, allowing it to guide us on our journey of healing, purpose, and abundant life in Him.

CHAPTER 12

LIVING WITH CONFIDENCE AND PURPOSE

As we come to the conclusion of this journey, it is essential to reflect on the key lessons and takeaways that have been explored throughout this book. In this final chapter, we will summarize the core principles and insights that can empower women to live with confidence and purpose. We will also offer encouragement and inspiration to readers, urging them to fully embrace their identity in Christ and step into their God-given purpose with boldness and conviction.

SUMMARIZING KEY LESSONS AND TAKEAWAYS:

Embracing Identity in Christ: Our true worth and purpose are found in our identity in Christ.

Throughout this book, we have emphasized the significance of understanding and embracing this truth. Recognizing that we are fearfully and wonderfully made, forgiven, and empowered by His Spirit sets the foundation for a life of confidence and purpose.

By overcoming false beliefs that hinder our self-worth, we can break free from the chains of comparison, perfectionism, and insecurity. Through introspection and the renewing of our minds, we challenge these misconceptions and replace them with God's truth. We come to understand that our worth is not determined by external measures, but by our identity in Christ.

As we embrace the healing and restoration that God offers, we let go of the pain, shame, and guilt that weigh us down. By surrendering our past wounds to Him, we allow His love to bring healing and transformation to our hearts. We learn to practice self-compassion, embracing our imperfections and forgiving ourselves as God has forgiven us. Through His love, we develop a healthy self-image based on His unconditional acceptance and grace.

Seeking God's will is a lifelong journey of seeking His guidance and aligning our lives with His plan. Through prayer, we communicate with Him, seeking His wisdom and direction. Through Scripture, we discover His principles and promises that guide our decisions and actions. Through discernment, we listen to the gentle nudges of the Holy Spirit, trusting that He will lead us in the path of purpose.

Understanding that our purpose unfolds in different seasons allows us to embrace the journey and trust in God's timing. We recognize that there may be times of waiting, growth, and transition, but in each season, we can find purpose and fulfillment. By aligning our lives with God's will, we walk in confidence, knowing that He has a unique plan for us and that every step we take is significant in His grand design.

As we overcome false beliefs, experience healing, and seek God's will, we come to embrace our true identity in Christ and live out our purpose with passion and confidence. We become vessels of His love, grace, and truth, impacting the world around us and bringing glory to His name.

EMBRACING YOUR IDENTITY IN CHRIST AND STEPPING INTO YOUR GOD-GIVEN PURPOSE:

As we conclude this book, I want to encourage you to fully embrace your identity in Christ and step into your God-given purpose with confidence and conviction. Remember that you are fearfully and wonderfully made, and that your worth is rooted in Him alone. Allow His love to heal your past wounds, develop a healthy self-image, and nurture a deep sense of purpose within you.

Take the lessons and insights you have gained and apply them to your daily life. Cultivate daily habits and spiritual disciplines that sustain your identity in Christ. Surround yourself with a supportive Christian community that encourages and uplifts you on your journey.

Seek God's guidance and align your life with His will.

Know that your life has immense value and significance. Your unique purpose aligns with God's Kingdom work, and you have the power to impact others in extraordinary ways. Step out in faith, embracing opportunities to serve, inspire, and influence those around you. Let your life be a testimony of God's love and truth.

Living with confidence and purpose is a lifelong pursuit. Embrace your identity in Christ, lean on His strength, and trust in His plans for your life. May you walk with confidence, live with purpose, and make a lasting impact on the world around you. May your life be a reflection of His love and bring glory to His name.

CHAPTER 13

SEEKING GOD'S WILL: STEPPING INTO YOUR TRUE IDENTITY

As we reach the final chapter of this book, we come to a crucial point in our journey. We have explored the depths of our identity in Christ, recognized the obstacles that hinder our growth, and discovered the transformative power of God's love. Now, it is time to take the next step—to seek God's will for our lives and step into our true identity through Him.

THE IMPORTANCE OF SEEKING GOD'S WILL:

Seeking God's will is not merely a religious exercise; it is a fundamental aspect of our faith journey. When we surrender our own desires and align ourselves with God's perfect plan, we position ourselves to experience His abundant blessings and fulfill our unique purpose. Seeking God's will allows us to walk in harmony with Him, trusting His guidance and relying on His wisdom.

LISTENING TO GOD'S VOICE:

To seek God's will, we must learn to listen to His voice. He speaks to us through His Word, prayer, and the still, small voice of the Holy Spirit. It is in the moments of quiet reflection and intimacy with God that we can discern His gentle nudges and guidance. By cultivating a deep relationship with Him, we become attuned to His leading and open to His direction.

DISCERNING GOD'S WILL:

Discerning God's will requires a combination of prayer, biblical wisdom, and wise counsel. We must seek His guidance in every aspect of our lives—our relationships, careers, ministries, and daily decisions. It is in the seeking that we find clarity and confidence to step into the path that God has laid out for us. As we study His Word and allow His principles to shape our thinking, we align our hearts with His and gain insight into His will.

PRACTICAL EXERCISES FOR SEEKING GOD'S WILL:

To help you on your journey of seeking God's will and stepping into your true identity, I offer you practical exercises and reflections:

Daily Surrender: Begin each day by surrendering your plans, desires, and ambitions to God. Invite Him to guide and direct your steps throughout the day.

Scriptural Meditation: Choose a passage of Scripture that speaks to seeking God's will, such as Proverbs 3:5-6 or Romans 12: Meditate on these verses, allowing them to renew your mind and align your thoughts with God's perspective.

Prayerful Reflection: Set aside intentional time for prayerful reflection, asking God to reveal His will to you. Listen for His voice, and journal your thoughts and impressions.

Seeking Wise Counsel: Seek out trusted mentors, pastors, or wise Christian friends who can provide guidance and support as you navigate important decisions. Their wisdom and insights can shed light on God's will for your life.

Stepping Out in Faith: As you discern God's will, be willing to step out in faith and take action. Trust that He will provide the necessary resources, strength, and guidance as you move forward.

AS WE CLOSE...

Dear reader, seeking God's will for your life and stepping into your true identity is a transformative and lifelong journey. It requires intentional effort, a humble heart, and a deep reliance on God's guidance. As you embark on this path, may you find profound insights, practical exercises, and biblical teachings in this book to be a compass guiding you towards a purposeful life aligned with God's plan.

Remember that God's will for your life is intricately connected to your unique identity in Him. He has a specific purpose and calling designed specifically for you. By seeking His will and embracing your true identity, you open the door to a life of meaning, impact, and fulfillment. May you walk boldly in the assurance that God's plan for you is perfect and that He will faithfully lead you every step of the way.

May this book serve as a resource and source of encouragement as you navigate the path towards living a purposeful life aligned with God's plan. May you continually seek His will, step into your true identity, and experience the joy and fulfillment that come from living a life that brings glory to Him. Trust in His guidance, lean on His promises, and embrace the adventure that awaits you as you walk hand in hand with your Heavenly Father.

Ways to Support!

PROPHETRENE.COM

$Rene4Ty

PProphetRene

@Prophet_Rene

@Prophet_Rene

ObadiahMinistries

Made in the USA
Columbia, SC
05 September 2023